T0209314

I AM
JONAH

Rediscovering God's Grace
in the Story of the Runaway Prophet

Brad Carr

WESTBOW
PRESS®
A DIVISION OF THOMAS NELSON
& ZONDERVAN

WestBow Press books may be ordered through booksellers or by contacting:

WestBow Press
A Division of Thomas Nelson & Zondervan
1663 Liberty Drive
Bloomington, IN 47403
www.westbowpress.com
844-714-3454

Because of the dynamic nature of the Internet, any web addresses or links contained in this book may have changed since publication and may no longer be valid. The views expressed in this work are solely those of the author and do not necessarily reflect the views of the publisher, and the publisher hereby disclaims any responsibility for them.

Any people depicted in stock imagery provided by Getty Images are models, and such images are being used for illustrative purposes only. Certain stock imagery © Getty Images.

All passages from the book of Jonah are the author's own translations.

Scripture quotations are taken from the Holy Bible, NEW INTERNATIONAL VERSION®, NIV® Copyright © 1973, 1978, 1984, 2011 by Biblica, Inc.® Used by permission. All rights reserved worldwide.

ISBN: 979-8-3850-0302-0 (sc)
ISBN: 979-8-3850-0282-5 (e)

Library of Congress Control Number: 2023913153

Print information available on the last page.

WestBow Press rev. date: 08/08/2023

Brad writes with the heart of a pastor and the mind of a scholar. He will lead you deeply into the story of Jonah, but he won't let you drown in the text. In every chapter he'll deliver you safely onto the dry ground of practical, real-life application. This book rescues Jonah from being only a children's story and shows how we can see ourselves in the life of this reluctant prophet at every stage of our faith journey. If you think you know the story of Jonah, this book will prove that God can reveal new treasure in the most familiar places and that his Word is always living and active in our lives.

Reuben Munn, Senior Pastor, Shore Community Church, Auckland, New Zealand

I first heard the messages found in this book when Brad preached through the book of Jonah at Summit Church in 2018. Then and now I am in awe of the way Brad creatively and skillfully opens our eyes to the often-missed layers in the story of Jonah and the convicting reality that 'I am Jonah.' You will not regret lingering with this book. You'll not only understand why you need Jesus – you'll also (re)discover the incredible character of our great God – his compassion, his kindness, his goodness, his graciousness, and his overflowing love.

Mel Palmer, Connections and Online Pastor, Gracecity Church, Auckland, New Zealand

I've been in pastoral ministry for more than 20 years and have preached Jonah twice and all I can say is, "I wish I had this book sooner!" *I Am Jonah* is exceptionally written, digs deeps into the story and personalizes the book in a way I haven't seen before. This is a must read for anyone approaching the book of Jonah!

Drew Leaver, Lead Pastor, Northeast Bible Church, San Antonio TX, United States

Brad gives such a compelling and exciting look into the adventures of this wayward prophet, showing the subtle hints from the Biblical text as to why Jonah seemingly never acknowledges his mistakes and his sins but is prepared to condemn others and pass judgement on them. For a Biblical story that is only 4 chapters, Brad opens the narrative up in such a way that one can fully grasp the cultural context, the motivations of the prophet, and the supernatural descriptions all in one book. We are invited to self-introspect at the end of every chapter, and clearly see how we have been like Jonah, and how we can respond positively to get our attitudes and motivations in line with the will of God and the call of God upon our lives. **Leonard Elisha Skumba, Pastor, Glad Tidings Fellowship, Harare, Zimbabwe**

If we're honest, many of us avoid reading the Bible because of the very real fear that God will use it to confront and change us. Rather than heeding God's voice and walking toward him, our natural bent is to run from him. In *I am Jonah* Brad serves us by not only highlighting our disposition that, like Jonah's, is to flee from God, but he also points us to our gracious God who calls, forgives, and unrelentingly pursues us with grace. An encouraging and challenging book. **Dr Malcolm Gill, Lead Pastor, Multicultural Bible Ministry, Sydney, Australia**

This is a remarkable little book. It satisfies both one's desire for solid biblical interpretation and one's desire for rich, life altering application. If you want to teach or preach through Jonah, this book will be invaluable to you. Or, if you simply want to understand more about this little story tucked away in the Old Testament, you'll find Brad's explanation invigorating and enlightening. Ultimately, I think reading *I Am Jonah* will help you love Jesus more and because of that, I can't recommend it to you highly enough. **Dr. Jeff Bucknam, Lead Pastor of Teaching and Vision, Harvest Bible Chapel, Chicago IL, United States**

There is so much of Jonah's reflection staring back at me as I read this book. While I may not *flee* like Jonah did, I have failed to *front up* with God's radical grace — too many times. Brad helps us see the Jonah in all of us. With a solid biblical framework, pastoral sensitively, and life application, this is a timely word from a timeless book. Believe me, you will never read the Jonah story in the same way again. **Jonathan Dove, Senior Pastor, Gracecity Church, Auckland, New Zealand**

Brad insightfully shines the spotlight on aspects of Jonah's character that are perhaps not immediately obvious to the everyday reader. Once he has us realizing how flawed Jonah was, Brad then skillfully shifts the spotlight onto the parts of our own hearts that also need some work. Brad's gentle and humble way, though incredibly convicting, encouraged, inspired, and gently guided me into greater obedience to the Lord.

Jenny Gill, Senior Pastor, The Street Church, Wellington, New Zealand

I Am Jonah is not just another book to be added on the readers' shelf, but a mirror to check our own inner self. Throughout the pages of this book, every reader will have an encounter with their crooked, disobedient and merciless self; but also with a gracious God. Brad authenticates this by beautifully and honestly integrating his first-hand stories into the message of the book of Jonah. *I Am Jonah* is not just a commentary, but a confidence on the God who graciously and relentlessly pursues after us even when we deliberately run away, disobey and are merciless toward others. Every reader will appreciate God's grace more every day because we are Jonah all day long.

Dr Ananda Tamang, Senior Pastor, Himalayan Isai Mandali Church, Lalitpur, Nepal

Brad artfully brings the story of Jonah to life the way God meant it to be shared, where we find ourselves in the story as strugglers and doubters and imperfect followers who are patiently loved by God toward a better existence if we are open to his work in our lives. I was both challenged and deeply encouraged in a way that will positively alter the trajectory of the rest of my life. I recommend jumping into the adventure of this book, which really is what it will feel like, in hopes that you will emerge different than when you embarked on the journey.

Jeff Jones, Lead Pastor, Chase Oaks Church, Plano TX, United States

To my wife Rochelle
as we approach thirty years of marriage,
having spent almost all that time
together in Christian ministry.
While I am the "on-stage" and visible one,
I can honestly say that everything
we have done in ministry we've done as a team.
Thank you honey for your love, encouragement, and belief
through all our adventures.

And to Daniel and Shih-Mei Lee,
for your encouragement and generosity in making this book happen.
Thank you for urging me to begin writing for a wider audience,
for your confidence that I could do it,
and for your support to make it happen.
I'm not sure I would have done this without you.

Contents

Foreword

Some readers love a fresh telling of the biblical narrative that engages the heart and touches the soul. They long to feel the Holy Spirit move as the story of the Bible comes alive and jolts their imagination. These lovers of Jesus want to be captured by the staggering presence of the Almighty God in the ancient world **and** in our lives today.

To these brothers and sisters, I say, the book you hold in your hands is true to the biblical narrative but will capture your heart in exciting new ways. You will feel what Jonah felt and encounter Yahweh in the pages of this book. You will identify with the ancient prophet so deeply that you will find yourself saying, for better or for worse, "I am Jonah!"

Other students of Scripture hunger for academic insight and rich theological reflection. They gravitate toward commentaries and historical works that unpack deep insight to cultural context and linguistic nuance. These people are inspired to love and follow God as their minds are enlivened with fresh insight and their understanding is expanded by digging deep into the richness of God's Word.

To these readers I say, consume this book and you will have great teaching to chew on and truth to digest. It will expand your mind and increase your knowledge.

There is another group of readers who love to be moved to action. They know that God is as alive today as he was in the ancient world when Jonah lived. These faithful followers of Jesus long to feel the Spirit of the Living God stir them to action and unleash world-transforming power through them. Nothing satisfies these believers more than being moved to holy engagement!

To these hungry world-changers I say, brace yourselves! *I Am Jonah* will challenge and move you to a Jesus-honoring lifestyle that will delight God and shake the world around you.

Most books do a great job speaking to *one* of these three audiences: those who long to feel God touch their *heart*, those who delight when their *mind* is fully engaged, and those who hunger for meaningful *life-change*. In this book, Brad Carr has done an artful job of weaving together all three of these groups of readers.

I have known Brad for over a decade and have had the honor of sitting under his teaching. Every time he speaks or writes, he opens the Scriptures with the heart of a pastor and the mind of a scholar. You can be confident that as you read this book, God will touch your heart, activate your mind, and transform your life.

Rev. Dr. Kevin G. Harney

President and Founder of Organic Outreach International

Lead Pastor of Shoreline Community Church

Author of the *Organic Outreach Trilogy* and *Organic Disciples*

Prologue

Welcome to my story.

I am Jonah.

Many have wondered why I chose to put my story into writing. After all, it doesn't provide a very flattering picture of me.

Who wants the whole world to know how disobedient you were to the call of God?

Who wants to remind people that a prophet of Yahweh refused to obey His call, and instead ran the other way?

Who wants other people to see the depths of selfishness in your heart?

Who wants others to listen to your private conversations with God, when you rant and argue about God's gracious love?

The truth is, left to myself, I probably wouldn't want you to know these things about me. And yet I have chosen to write my story.

Why? Two reasons.

First, I sense the call of God to write it. I am a prophet of Yahweh, a servant of the God of Israel. I am called to teach and proclaim His law and love, His wrath and mercy. And I believe that this story is a stunning revelation of the gracious character of Yahweh.

The second reason is that God's people need it, not just my generation of Israelites, but also generations of believers to come. The truth is, I am not unique—God's people have shown a remarkable tendency through the ages to ignore His call, run from His presence, take His grace for granted, and rant when things don't go their way.

My sense is that you need to hear my story.

You need to find yourself in it.

And in doing so, you will rediscover the awe-inspiring grace of God.

So enjoy my tale. But rather than it simply being a window into my story, let it be a mirror into your own.

Introduction: A Great Story

Before our first son, Harrison, was born, we purchased or were given small books of Bible stories. Some were made out of soft fabric, while others were thick cardboard. All of them were filled with bright colors and vivid pictures and were resilient enough to be gnawed on with toothless gums.

As each of our three sons came along, these were the first Bible stories they heard.

Each collection of stories was drawn from the best-known accounts in scripture:

David and Goliath.

Daniel in the lions' den.

Jesus feeding the crowd of five thousand people.

And the story of Jonah and the big fish.

The tale of Jonah is among the best-known narratives in the Bible. And yet at the same time, I will argue it's also one of the least understood.

I have known and loved this story for as long as I can remember. Growing up in a church-going family, Jonah is one of the earliest Bible characters whom I knew. As a young teenager, our youth group performed a musical based on this narrative. And then when I came to Hebrew classes in seminary, Jonah was one of the books that we practiced our rudimentary skills on.

And yet, when I came to preach through the book of Jonah in our church, I was still surprised at how little I had understood the primary message of this story.

And I was surprised how powerfully this message hit home to those who sat through those sermons.

Now having preached through Jonah a second time with another congregation and spent copious hours soaking in its richness, I am offering this short book that seeks to unpack the beauty of this exquisite yet challenging story.

As we prepare to immerse ourselves in Jonah's story, let me make four brief observations about the narrative.

It's a Challenging Story

As we begin Jonah's tale, we need to understand that it will be an immensely challenging journey.

That's because this book isn't simply about Jonah.

It's about all of us.

As suggested in the prologue, I believe that the book of Jonah is intended to be a mirror into our own lives, our own struggles with God, and our own tendencies to run from Him.[1]

Traditionally, the book of Jonah is read aloud in Jewish synagogues on the holy day of Yom Kippur—the Day of Atonement.[2] Different synagogues personalize the way they then invite their congregations to respond to this ancient story. In some synagogues, when the reading comes to the end of the narrative, the congregation then stand together and confess in unison, "We are Jonah."[3]

That is where the title of this book comes from—"I Am Jonah."

Why? Because you and I are exactly like this ancient prophet.

We ignore God's commands.

We run in disobedience.

We say we believe and worship the God of heaven, while our lives and actions proclaim something different.

We give thanks for God's amazing grace and then refuse to pass on that grace and forgiveness to others.

We pursue comfort over mission.

We are Jonah.

The book of Jonah is a brilliantly written narrative that invites you to witness the failings of a wayward prophet, and then just as you're shaking your head in despair at his foolishness, the spotlight is turned back on you.

The window into Jonah's life becomes a mirror into your own.

I am Jonah.

And so are you.

In light of that, at the end of each chapter in this book, there is a concluding section entitled "I Am Jonah." There, having watched

Jonah miss God's grace again and again, we will pause and reflect on the different ways we can be just like him.

There is also a brief prayer of confession that I invite you to use as you talk with our gracious, heavenly Father.

It's a Vulnerable Story

The reason that Jonah's tale is so challenging is its vulnerability.

Strictly speaking, the book of Jonah is an anonymous work. Unlike a number of other biblical books that mention their authors by name (e.g., Isaiah 1:1), no one is explicitly named as the author.

My belief, however, is that Jonah almost certainly wrote his story.[4]

How else would an anonymous author have known about the events on the boat in the middle of the ocean (Jonah 1:4–16)? How would anyone else know the content of Jonah's prayer inside the great fish (Jonah 2:1–9)?

It is certainly possible, I suppose, that Jonah could have shared the story with someone else who wrote it all down. It's also possible that God could have simply revealed the whole story to someone else.

But many of the Old Testament prophets wrote down both the prophetic words they received from God and some of the narratives and events surrounding those oracles.[5]

Is it so hard to believe that a well-known prophet like Jonah[6] would have written down the story of what God revealed to him?

And if this is Jonah's story that he himself carefully crafted, it is amazingly vulnerable.

As we will see shortly, the book of Jonah is a satire or parody where Jonah, as the chief character, acted in completely unexpected ways that end up making him look silly. But if Jonah is indeed the author, this means that he deliberately wrote his story this way, knowing that he would end up looking ridiculous but also knowing how powerful it would be in challenging and transforming the lives of its readers.

This is the power of vulnerability.

> Pretending to be invulnerable fails, producing lives suffocated by fear and shame … Only by being more honest, more open, and more realistic about our struggles and limits can we experience any sense of wholeness.[7]

Jonah's vulnerability invites us to be more open and honest about our failings, struggles, and shortcomings as we read his story.

Time after time as I have written and re-written these chapters, I have found myself shaking my head at my own foolishness as well as Jonah's.

That's the power of Jonah's vulnerability.

And in the end, that's what makes his story so challenging.

It's a Beautiful Story

Part of the reason Jonah's vulnerability carries such a punch is that his story is so brilliantly written.

One of the mistakes we can make as we approach the book of Jonah is to assume that it is a simple little tale that is great for bedtime reading with children but has little to teach adults.

The fact is that the book of Jonah is a beautiful and complex piece of literature, as well as a theologically rich and challenging part of the Bible.

The fabric of the narrative has been wonderfully woven together.

As mentioned earlier, one of the key ways this is done is through the use of satire or parody. Satire is a comical, tongue-in-cheek way of telling a story, and this book is full of it. One scholar calls Jonah "the greatest satiric masterpiece in the Bible."[8]

Time and time again, we will see how Jonah's actions end up being the opposite of what we expect, in a way that makes him look quite ridiculous.

As one of my professors puts it, "You're supposed to smile as you read this book."[9]

This brilliant use of satire and irony throughout the story is one of the major ways its message is driven home.

Another feature of the book is the use of key words that carry the story along and tie it all together. For example, one of the most important words in the book is the Hebrew term *gadol*, normally translated "great." It is used fourteen times throughout the story to describe key objects such as the powerful city of Nineveh, the object of God's loving grace (six times). It is also used in the book to describe elements such as the great wind (Jonah 1:4), the great storm (Jonah 1:4), and the great fish (Jonah 1:17).[10]

The use of this adjective helps enlarge the story in our imagination as it unfolds. It helps make the book come alive and contributes to its comical style.

This is why I have chosen to use the word *great* in the title of each chapter in this book.

Finally, there is a beautiful symmetry to the book that carries the story along. It has two parallel sections, each with two scenes that mirror the other.

These sections and scenes follow almost completely the chapter divisions in our modern Bibles.[11]

The opening scenes in each section, chapters 1 and 3, *mirror* each other in very precise ways as Jonah first disobeys and then obeys the call of God. In both of these chapters, he ends up preaching to pagans, and they come to faith in God.

The subsequent scenes, in chapters 2 and 4, then *contrast* with each other as Jonah responds to God's gracious salvation work with either thanks or lament.

The structure of the book therefore looks like this:

Section One	Section Two
Jonah 1—A Great Storm	**Jonah 3—A Great City**
God calls.	God calls (again).
Jonah runs.	Jonah obeys.
God pursues and saves.	God pursues and saves.
Pagan sailors believe.	Pagan Ninevites believe.
Jonah 2—A Great Prayer	**Jonah 4—A Great Lesson**
A grateful prophet prays a psalm of thanks.	An angry prophet prays prayers of lament.

Other literary features will be highlighted as we work our way through the story.

For now, however, we simply need to be aware that Jonah is not just a simple little tale. It is, in fact, an exquisite literary masterpiece.

It's a True Story

Finally, not only is the book of Jonah a *challenging, vulnerable,* and *beautiful* story but I also believe we need to appreciate it as a true story.[12]

Over the past few centuries, many people have chosen to question and reject the historical reliability of the Bible. And one of the key books in this battle has been this story of Jonah.

For many people in our modern world, the concept of a person being swallowed whole by a big fish, remaining alive within the fish for three days, and then being vomited back out again ready to carry on with life, is preposterous.

A fairy tale.

An urban legend.

One more fishing story that got out of hand.

Just another whale of a tale.

My response is simply that a person's acceptance of the truthfulness of this story comes down to whether they believe that miracles are possible.

If there is a God who stands outside the cosmos as the all-powerful Creator and who steps into His creation in different ways that can suspend the normal laws of nature, then miracles can take place.

If there isn't an all-powerful Creator, then miracles can't happen.

And as far as miracles go, the miracle of Jonah surviving inside a fish for three days is hardly spectacular. Many other miracles of the Bible, such as an entire nation crossing the Red Sea on dry land[13] or Joshua asking God to stop the rotation of the earth so that the sun would appear to stand still,[14] seem far bigger hurdles to jump over.

Not to mention the greatest miracle of all—the resurrection of Jesus Christ from the dead.

So if a person thinks the Bible is just a collection of ancient stories and myths that have little historical value, they will undoubtedly reject the book of Jonah as a fable or myth.

If, on the other hand, a person believes that God is real, that He performs miraculous events in history, and that the greatest miracle of all is that Jesus rose physically and bodily from the dead, then that person should have no difficulty in accepting the book of Jonah as historically true.[15]

In addition, it should be noted that the story doesn't even major on the miracle of the fish.

Despite the common "Jonah and the Whale" title, the great fish is *not* an important part of the story (and it isn't even necessarily a whale— it's just called "a great fish"). In literary terms, the fish is not a major character (even though we have put a fish on the cover of this book!).

As we will see later in the book, the fish is only mentioned in three verses (Jonah 1:17; 2:1, 10) in a way that frames and sets the scene for Jonah's prayer in chapter 2. And this is completely different from the way legends or myths generally work. If this was myth or legend, then the story about the fish would usually be highly embellished to draw attention to it. Instead of this, the author simply records what has taken place in minimal fashion and moves on.[16]

In the end, then, I have found that people's willingness to accept the book of Jonah as a true account of actual events doesn't depend on the fish.

It rests on their willingness to accept the historical truth of the Bible.

So rather than getting distracted by the fish, we are better to take the story as it is written—a narrative describing real events that have actually taken place that has a great deal to teach us. And instead of focusing on the fish, we should be looking at other key characters in the story.

As one writer has put it, "Men have been looking so hard at the great fish that they have failed to see the great God."[17]

That's exactly what this book is designed to help us do—come face-to-face with the awe-inspiring grace of an incredible God.

Chapter 1: A Great Call
(Jonah 1:1–3)

Now the word of Yahweh came to Jonah son of Amittai, saying,
"Get up and go to the great city of Nineveh and proclaim against it,
because their evil has risen up to me."
But Jonah got up and ran away to Tarshish, far away from Yahweh.

Jonah 1:1–3a

The book of Jonah is one of the twelve shorter texts at the end of the Old Testament that are commonly lumped together as the Minor Prophets.[18] This term is meant to suggest something about their length when compared with the other prophetic writings of Isaiah, Jeremiah, Ezekiel, and Daniel (the so-called Major Prophets).

Unfortunately, this term often seems to reflect something more than just their length.

For many people, it seems to sum up a lack of importance to their spiritual walk. How many people have ever selected a "life verse" from Obadiah or Nahum?[19] These books parked at the end of our Old Testament, are often deemed to be quite irrelevant for modern followers of Jesus.

Others might assume that the term *Minor Prophets* refers to the musical key in which they would be sung. These prophetic writings are often deemed to be dark and depressing, to be sung in a minor key. They are filled with oracles and visions of God's judgment being poured out on unrepentant sinners.

So it's not surprising that, for many people, these Minor Prophets are uncharted, unfamiliar territory.

Apart from Jonah.

While many Christians will struggle to provide meaningful information about the lives or messages of the other eleven minor prophets, many believers can sketch the basic storyline of the book of Jonah. Even people who have never read the Bible have heard something about Jonah and the big fish.

The book of Jonah seems to stand apart from the other eleven, almost as though it doesn't quite fit with the rest of them.

And in many ways, that is true.

Unlike all the other writings of the prophets, Jonah contains no written oracles from God of either blessing or judgment (apart from his brief sermon in Nineveh in Jonah 3:4).

Unlike the others, Jonah records no great visions.

There are no detailed prophecies of doom for God's people if they don't repent.

Neither are there stirring oracles of a future hope and kingdom.

Unlike all the other prophetic books, Jonah is simply written as a narrative, as a story.[20] And that's why it's known so well—we're a lot more comfortable reading a story like Jonah's than navigating the apocalyptic visions of the other minor prophets.

But while we may think we know Jonah's story, I think we are going to be in for a surprise.

An Unsurprising Beginning

Having just made the case that the book of Jonah is quite unlike the other prophetic books, it starts off in a very similar way. The opening words of Jonah 1:1 are relatively standard in the prophetic writings: "Now the word of Yahweh came to Jonah son of Amittai, saying ..."

A number of the prophetic books start with the same formula. For example, the book of Hosea begins, "The word of the LORD [Yahweh] that came to Hosea son of Beeri" (Hosea 1:1).[21]

This was the standard way a prophet reported a message or oracle they had received from God.[22]

And it wasn't just the writing prophets who received "the word of Yahweh." Key characters through the Old Testament—such as Abraham, Moses, Samuel, Nathan, and Solomon—were also said to explicitly have received "the word of Yahweh" at different points in their lives and ministries.[23]

Yahweh, by the way, is the name of the God of the Bible. When God revealed Himself in the burning bush to Moses in the book of Exodus, He said,

> Say to the Israelites, "The LORD [Yahweh], the God of your fathers—the God of Abraham, the God of Isaac and the God of Jacob—has sent me to you.
>
> > This is my name for ever,
> > the name you shall call me
> > from generation to generation." (Exodus 3:15)

3

Brad Carr

God's name, *Yahweh*, is used almost seven thousand times throughout the Old Testament,[24] particularly when the authors wanted to emphasize God's covenant with the nation of Israel and His unfailing love for them. So when the writers of scripture wanted to highlight the greatness and power of God as Creator, they would tend to use His title *Elohim*, which we translate as "God." But when they wanted to emphasize His compassionate and gracious love for His people, they would call Him by name, *Yahweh*.

The problem is that almost all our English translations follow the ancient Jewish tradition of substituting the title "the Lord" (in small caps) in place of "Yahweh" to ensure they did not unintentionally break the third commandment about misusing His name (Exodus 20:7).

My belief, however, based on His command to Moses in Exodus 3:15, is that Yahweh actually wants us to know and use His name.

So whenever I translate a portion of the story of Jonah through this book, I will use the divine name *Yahweh* where the Hebrew text does.

And when I quote from other parts of the Old Testament, using the NIV translation, I will add "Yahweh" in brackets when the NIV uses "the Lord."[25]

So "the word of Yahweh" was a divine revelation that a person received from Yahweh, the God of Israel. And many times, that recipient was recognized as a prophet of Yahweh.

That is certainly true of Jonah.

Outside of the book that bears his name, and the gospels in the New Testament that record Jesus's references to Jonah, the only other mention of him in the Bible is found in the second book of Kings.

He [King Jeroboam] was the one who restored the boundaries of Israel from Lebo Hamath to the Dead Sea, in accordance with the word of the LORD [Yahweh], the God of Israel, spoken through his servant Jonah son of Amittai, the prophet from Gath Hepher. (2 Kings 14:25)

So it seems that Jonah was a recognized prophet of Yahweh in the northern kingdom of Israel.[26] Almost two hundred years before Jonah's time, the nation of Israel had split into two separate kingdoms upon the death of King Solomon. The southern kingdom of Judah was centered in Jerusalem and was still ruled by the descendants of King David. The northern kingdom, made up of ten of the original tribes, was ruled from the city of Samaria but had fluctuated under several different rulers and dynasties.

Jonah grew up in the northern kingdom of Israel, and 2 Kings tells us that he was raised in Gath Hepher. According to Joshua 19:13, this town was part of the tribal lands of Zebulun, in the area that later came to be called Galilee. In fact, Gath Hepher was just a few miles from the town of Nazareth, meaning that, in different times, Jonah and Jesus grew up in the same backyard.[27]

Of all the rulers of this northern kingdom, King Jeroboam II was probably the most successful politically and militarily, and he was able to expand the borders of the kingdom to their greatest extent. However, like all his northern predecessors, he was not a follower of Yahweh, and some of Jonah's contemporaries, such as Hosea and Amos, condemned the unjust and immoral practices of Jeroboam's regime. For example:

> They delight the king with their wickedness,
> the princes with their lies.
> They are all adulterers,
> burning like an oven

whose fire the baker need not stir
from the kneading of the dough till it rises.
On the day of the festival of our king
the princes become inflamed with wine,
and he joins hands with the mockers. (Hosea 7:3–5)

For three sins of Israel,
even for four, I will not relent.
They sell the innocent for silver,
and the needy for a pair of sandals.
They trample on the heads of the poor
as on the dust of the ground
and deny justice to the oppressed.
Father and son use the same girl
and so profane my holy name.
They lie down beside every altar
on garments taken in pledge.
In the house of their god
they drink wine taken as fines. (Amos 2:6–8)

However, no such words of condemnation or judgment seem to have come from the mouth of Jonah.

Rather, from the little information we have, it seems as though Jonah may have supported and encouraged the expansion of Israel under Jeroboam's leadership. It may be that "the original readers of the book of Jonah would have remembered him as intensely patriotic, a highly partisan nationalist."[28]

This makes it all the more surprising that it is Jonah, and not one of his contemporaries, who receives this unexpected mission from Yahweh.

A Surprising Message

While the opening verse of the book of Jonah is standard prophetic fare, the next verse is dynamite: "Get up and go to the great city of Nineveh and proclaim against it, because their evil has risen up to me" (Jonah 1:2).

This is a huge surprise for two reasons.

First, no other prophet had ever been asked to travel outside the kingdoms of Israel and Judah to preach.[29]

Some of the prophets did proclaim messages against foreign nations. For example, the prophet Isaiah was a contemporary of Jonah, preaching in the southern kingdom of Judah. He pronounced some startling oracles of judgment against several countries including Assyria, Babylon, Philistia, and Egypt.[30] Amos, another contemporary, did a similar thing, as would Jeremiah, Obadiah, and Nahum in the coming years.[31]

However, none of them were ever commanded by God to specifically *go* to those nations. When they proclaimed messages against foreign nations, the prophets of Yahweh did so from the relative safety of home.

In other words, they were simply commanded to "preach" or "proclaim."

Only Jonah is told "*go* ... and proclaim."

That was an unprecedented as well as an unwelcome call.

The second reason why this call is a huge surprise is that Jonah was sent to *Nineveh*. Of all the foreign places to be sent to, the last nation on the earth any Israelite would wish to travel to in Jonah's day was the kingdom of Assyria and its notorious city.

The Assyrians were the Nazis of the ancient world.

Archaeologists have uncovered huge stone reliefs that depict in grotesque art how the merciless kings of Assyria glorified their victories over conquered peoples. These reliefs and accompanying narratives boast of brutalities such as live dismemberment, beheadings, live skinning of victims, eye-gouging, and pulling out of tongues. They would burn young boys and girls alive. There are pictures of great piles of heads, feet, and hands taken from captives, as well as multiple heads impaled on stakes.

One scholar describes the Assyrians as "terror-mongers,"[32] the original terrorist state.

One Assyrian king, Ashurnasirpal II, writing a few years before Jonah's time, boasted,

> I flayed as many nobles as had rebelled against me [and] draped their skins over the pile [of corpses] ... I burnt their adolescent boys [and] girls ... I captured many troops alive: I cut off some of their arms [and] hands; I cut off of others their noses, ears, [and] extremities. I gouged out the eyes of many troops ... I hung their heads on trees around the city.[33]

You can see why I liken them to Adolf Hitler's Nazis. Jewish writer Hayyim Lewis agrees, writing,

> The Assyrians were the Nazi storm-troopers of the ancient world ... They showed no quarter in battle, uprooting entire peoples in their fury for conquest ... For Jonah, Nineveh ... stood as a symbol of evil incarnate.[34]

It is no wonder that Yahweh said to Jonah, "their evil has risen up to me" (Jonah 1:2).

More than a century after Jonah, the prophet Nahum fired this broadside from Yahweh at this brutal nation:[35]

> Woe to the city of blood,
>   full of lies,
> full of plunder,
>   never without victims!
> The crack of whips,
>   the clatter of wheels,
> galloping horses
>   and jolting chariots!
> Charging cavalry,
>   flashing swords
>   and glittering spears!
> Many casualties,
>   piles of dead,
> bodies without number,
>   people stumbling over the corpses. (Nahum 3:1–3)

Why do I emphasise at length the brutality and horror of the Assyrian hordes in Nineveh?

Simply because, as I read books about Jonah, I see so many authors sitting in judgment on this prophet and what he is about to do in the next verse (Jonah 1:3).

So before we casually condemn Jonah for his actions, we need to understand the utter shock and surprise caused by the call of Yahweh.

To ask a Jewish prophet to proclaim the judgment of Yahweh in Nineveh will be like transporting him into the twentieth century and asking him to go and preach against the sin and tyranny of the Nazis themselves in Berlin, Germany, in the late 1930s.

A Shocking Response

While the command of Yahweh to proclaim His word in Nineveh would have been a complete surprise to Jonah, his response to the divine command was an utter shock.

He ran.

And he ran far, far away.

Jonah didn't just run to the end of the street like a petulant child and hid in the bushes for a few hours. Jonah's plan was to run as far from Nineveh—and Yahweh—as he could.

> This type of rebellion is something recorded of no other prophet of the Lord.[36]

Verses 2–3 mention three geographical locations that are important if we are to fully understand Jonah's intention to escape.

> Go to the great city of *Nineveh* ... But Jonah got up and ran away to *Tarshish*, far away from Yahweh. He went down to *Joppa*, and he found a ship bound for Tarshish, and he paid the fare, and went down into it to sail to *Tarshish*, far away from Yahweh. (emphasis added)

The first location is, of course, *Nineveh*. On a map, this pagan city was over 500 miles north-east of Israel.

The second location is *Joppa* (modern Jaffa), one of the nearest seaports to Israel but controlled for centuries by the Philistines, the ancient enemies of Israel. For Israelites, Joppa was one of the main gateways to the Mediterranean Sea and the lands beyond.

The third location is *Tarshish*, the destination across the sea where Jonah was headed. Most scholars believe that Tarshish was in modern Spain,[37] around 2,500 miles west of Israel.

In other words, Jonah was running in the opposite direction to Nineveh, and as far away as he could get![38]

Verse 3 contains a number of important features that are easily missed if we read the story too quickly.

First, after the simple prose of the first two verses, verse 3 contains a number of verbs that almost tumble over one another in describing what Jonah did.

> He got up.
>
> He ran away.
>
> He went down.
>
> He found.
>
> He paid.
>
> He went down.
>
> He sailed.[39]

That's a lot of verbs. The way this verse is written gives the impression that Jonah was moving fast. No hanging around. No surfing the internet looking at possible destinations and dream locations.

He didn't sell the house.

He didn't sort out the furniture.

He didn't get someone to look after the dog.

He just ran, and he ran as fast as he could.

The second thing to notice in verse 3 is what Jonah didn't do.

He didn't pray. He didn't talk to Yahweh about his fears or concerns.

This will become even more apparent when we get into the rest of chapter 1, when the ship was in the midst of a fierce storm, and everyone on board was praying to their gods—except Jonah.

Jonah contrasts sharply here with other biblical characters.

For example, Moses was terrified when he was called at the burning bush in Exodus 3. He had left Egypt forty years before as an abject failure, running for his life. And then Yahweh called him to go back to Egypt to lead Israel out of slavery. Exodus 3 and 4 contain a fascinating dialogue between Moses and Yahweh, as Moses raised no less than five objections about why he was not the right choice to lead Israel out of Egypt.

The prophet Jeremiah also pushed back when he was called by God as a prophet, arguing he was much too young for such a commission (see Jeremiah 1:6).

The contrast here with Jonah is stark.

Jonah didn't pray.

He didn't debate.

He didn't share his fears or concerns or objections.

He just ran.

Third, notice the precise wording of verse 3. Jonah was undoubtedly fleeing *from Nineveh*. He was headed in the opposite direction geographically from where God had told him to go. But twice in verse 3, we are told *whom* Jonah was really running from: "But Jonah got up and ran ... *far away from Yahweh* ... he went down into it to sail to Tarshish, *far away from Yahweh*." (emphasis added)

Jonah wasn't just running from *Nineveh*.

He was running from *Yahweh*.

It seemed as though he had forgotten the words of Psalm 139:7-10.[40]

> Where can I go from your Spirit?
>> Where can I flee from your presence?
> If I go up to the heavens, you are there;
>> if I make my bed in the depths, you are there.
> If I rise on the wings of the dawn,
>> if I settle on the far side of the sea,
> even there your hand will guide me,
>> your right hand will hold me fast.

The fourth observation may not be immediately obvious, but as chapter 1 unfolded Jonah took a series of downward steps.[41]

In verse 3 he went "down to Joppa." This was partly a geographical term as most of Israel was hill country, so when a person travelled to the coast, they would travel downhill.

But it also seemed to have moral overtones, showing the downward direction that Jonah's life was taking.

Later in verse 5, we will see that Jonah went down into the boat to sleep. At the end of the chapter, he would be thrown overboard and go down into the water until, finally, he would say that he went down "to the bottom of the mountains" (Jonah 2:6), "into the heart of the seas" (Jonah 2:3).

And this all leads us to the key idea of these opening verses in the story of Jonah:

Running from God may seem easy, but it's always a downward journey.

One of the lies of our enemy is that when we choose to turn our back on God and disobey His commands, our lives will be so much better. That was the heart of the lie to our first parents in the Garden of Eden. The serpent whispered to Eve, "For God knows that when you eat from it your eyes will be opened, and you will be like God, knowing good and evil" (Genesis 3:5).

But as the rest of Genesis 3, and indeed the rest of the Bible, makes clear, that is not true. The story of the Bible went downhill after they reached out, took the fruit, and ate it.

Jonah's story suggested that as well. The decision to run from God was the beginning of a tragic descent.

Running from God may seem easy, but it's always a downward journey.

It's possible that for Jonah, it did look all too easy.

He ran to the nearest port, and there he just happened to find a ship that was ready to sail. And the captain just happened to be willing to take a paying passenger along with the rest of the cargo. And it just happened that the ship was heading to where he wanted to go, to Tarshish—in the exact opposite direction to Nineveh.

Pastor J. D. Greear has observed, "If you want to disobey, there will always be a ship prepared to take you to Tarshish."[42]

If your marriage is struggling and you want to have an affair, the enemy will always make sure there is someone attractive and available.

If you're in a conflict with someone and you would rather gossip to a third party instead of working hard to forgive, there will always be someone to listen across the café table.

If you are struggling with materialism and spending money on stuff to mask your pain, there will always be another mail-order catalog.

If you struggle with lust, there will always be another website to click on to.

There is a warning here for us. Many Christians go through life using the principle of the "open door." They will pray and ask God to open a door for them in an attempt to seek His will.

And at times, this is a very biblical concept.

The apostle Paul asked his friends in Colossae to pray that God would open a door by providing an opportunity to evangelize.[43]

Jesus Himself told the church in Philadelphia that He had placed an open door before them.[44]

However, it is wrong to assume that *every* opportunity in front of us is, therefore, an open door from God. Just because there happened to be a ship heading for Tarshish, tied up at the wharf in Joppa, didn't mean that was where Yahweh wanted Jonah to go.

Just because there is an opportunity, doesn't mean that God has provided an open door.

The final observation is not obvious in most of our English translations but is fascinating.

> Ancient Jewish tradition suggests that Jonah had to rent the entire ship for his journey.[45]

This interpretation is based on the fact that in the original Hebrew text, the fare or hirage is described with a feminine pronoun. A male pronoun will have suggested a translation of "his passage," referring to Jonah. Instead, a feminine pronoun can be translated as "her passage" and is probably a reference to the ship.

This would mean that Jonah was forced to pay for the entire ship and crew, rather than simply the cost of his own ticket.

Who said running away from God wasn't costly?

I Am Jonah

In the introduction, I suggested that Jonah's story is not meant to simply be a window into Jonah's life, but also to be a mirror into our own.

So at the end of each chapter, we will pause and reflect on how we can so often be exactly like him. As we come to the end of the opening verses from this amazing book, I will suggest four ways in which we can be exactly like Jonah.

1. I am Jonah when I say no to what God has clearly said.

Yahweh clearly says to His prophet Jonah, "Get up and go to the great city of Nineveh and preach against it." Jonah's problem is *not* that he doesn't hear or understand what God has said. His problem is that he doesn't like it.

It's the same with us today. We now hold the written Word of God, the Bible, in our hands. God clearly speaks to us in His Word. And like Jonah, our problem is not that we do not hear, but that sometimes we do not like what we hear.

God has clearly said, "Go and make disciples of all nations" (Matthew 28:19).

God has clearly said, "Flee from sexual immorality" (1 Corinthians 6:18).

God has clearly said, "Pray continually" (1 Thessalonians 5:17).

God has clearly said, "You shall not covet your neighbor's house" (Exodus 20:17).

God has clearly said, "Love your enemies, do good to those who hate you" (Luke 6:27).

God has clearly said, "Do not worry about tomorrow" (Matthew 6:34).

Our problem is not that we do not understand what God has said. Our problem is that we struggle to obey.

As Mark Twain once said, "It ain't the parts of the Bible *that I can't understand* that bother me, it's the parts *that I do understand*."

And whenever we fail to obey what God has clearly said, we are behaving exactly like Jonah.

This doesn't mean, of course, that we always leave town. Running from God can sometimes mean we stay in exactly the same place geographically—in the same town, at the same address, in the same job, part of the same family, attending the same church.

But in our hearts, we're running away.

In his superb book on this story entitled *The Prodigal Prophet*, author and pastor Tim Keller suggests that Jonah is like both of the sons in Jesus's classic parable of the lost sons in Luke 15. In the first two chapters of the story, Jonah is like the younger son who blatantly disobeys and runs from the father. But in the final two chapters of the book, Jonah is like the elder son, outwardly obedient while still resisting and disagreeing with the father.[46]

In a sense, both sons are running from the father.

But only one of them actually leaves home.

The same can be true of us. We may not run to the nearest seaport; we may not even leave the house. Our address may be exactly the same.

But we are just like Jonah when we say no to God.

2. I am Jonah when I resist God altering my life plans.

In her book on Jonah, entitled *Life Interrupted*, best-selling author Priscilla Shirer suggests that a big part of Jonah's problem might have been that God interrupted Jonah's cozy life. Jonah was comfortable and happy. As we saw in 2 Kings 14, Jonah had predicted this great expansion of the northern kingdom; he had announced God's blessing on the nation.

> Most likely, therefore, he was popular, highly respected, and greatly appreciated in his role … He was living the prophet's dream. And he was more than content for things to keep on going the way they'd always gone, the way he had planned

and fully expected they would. He was living for God, doing His work, and doing it well.[47]

And then God changed the script.

He altered the plan.

He tried to move Jonah onto a new ministry.

I am writing this book in the aftermath of suffering serious burnout. After sixteen years of pastoring the church that my wife, Rochelle, and I planted with a wonderful team, I needed to step down from leadership for the sake of my health and my mental and spiritual well-being. It was a tough decision, and at times in the following months, it was an even harder decision to live with.

But we firmly believe that while God did not cause the burnout, He has used it to call us into a new ministry. He has changed the plan that we thought we had been following for the next couple of decades. And our job now is to trust His plans and follow Him.

Whenever God alters the direction of our lives, whether through sickness or redundancy or new challenges or a fresh call, it can be hard.

And in those moments, we often end up questioning not just God's call and plan, but also His goodness.

Keller points out that while Jonah had a problem with the assignment that God had given him, he had an even bigger problem with God Himself. "Jonah doubted the goodness, wisdom, and justice of God."[48]

We do the same thing all the time.

Whenever we resist God's plan, ignore God's commands, or run from God's call, it is generally because we think we know better than Him. And that often stems from deep doubts about His character.

We doubt His heart.

We question His motives.

We're unsure about His love.

And so we resist His plan, His commands, and His call.

Because we know best, not God—right?

3. I am Jonah when I fail to talk to God.

In some ways, this observation follows on from the last one. When life does get altered, when God does interrupt our plans and change our direction, we often end up silent, just like Jonah.

This is where the contrast between Moses and Jonah is staggering when their stories are placed side by side.

Neither of these prophets liked the commission Yahweh gave them.

Neither of them wanted to go.

(Interestingly, both of them ended up going and being used by God.)

The key difference, however, is that Moses talked to God about how he was feeling. He raised his objections. Moses prayed.

Jonah didn't.

The truth is that we are often much more like Jonah than Moses. I have found in my own life that prayerlessness can be a frequent downfall. I have always struggled to pray consistently.

But that has been especially true when I have struggled with obedience, direction, or with difficult circumstances.

My tendency has often been to shut up shop for a while and stop praying.

Just like Jonah.

The constant call of scripture is to talk to God. We are commanded to pray continually about whatever we are facing.[49]

Paul wrote to the Philippians:

> Do not be anxious about anything, but in every situation, by prayer and petition, with thanksgiving, present your requests to God. And the peace of God, which transcends all understanding, will guard your hearts and your minds in Christ Jesus. (Philippians 4:5–6)

We'll come back to this topic again later in the book.

4. I am Jonah when I would rather be comfortable than obedient.

That's the bottom line, isn't it?

If we had to choose between a positive, well-received, well-respected ministry in our homeland and a new call to a land that hated our people and our God and skinned their victims alive, wouldn't most of us have run with Jonah?

Brad Carr

As UK pastor Phil Moore points out, "It is much harder to say, 'yes' to God when we are successful."[50]

Ultimately, it comes down to who is really in control of our lives.

Who's really in the driver's seat?

Most of us who are followers of Jesus want to say that God's in charge. He's the One calling the shots. We have no problem singing, 'I have decided to follow Jesus, no turning back.'

But the truth is that there are many times in life that we want to take control.

We want to grab the wheel.

We don't like where God is taking us or what He's calling us to do.

But the constant message of the Bible is that God is God, and we are not.

That's why the first of the famous Ten Commandments says, "You shall have no other gods before me" (Exodus 20:3).

That's why the lie of the evil one in the Garden of Eden was, "God knows that when you eat from it your eyes will be opened, and *you will be like God*" (Genesis 3:5; emphasis added).

That's why Jesus said, "Whoever wants to be my disciple must deny themselves and take up their cross and follow me" (Mark 8:34).

For the constant struggle for us sons and daughters of Adam and Eve is to want to play God and pretend that we're calling the shots.

God wants me to be obedient.

But I'd rather be comfortable.

I am Jonah.

---

1. I am Jonah when I say no to what God has clearly said.

2. I am Jonah when I resist God altering my life plans.

3. I am Jonah when I fail to talk to God.

4. I am Jonah when I would rather be comfortable than obedient.

Father,

I am Jonah.

It is very easy to read his story and shake my head at what Jonah does. But then I realize the book is just as much a mirror of my own life as a window into his. I have run from You so often in my life. I have run whenever I have chosen not to obey what You have said. I have been like Jonah when I have resisted Your plans for my life. I am like him when I forget or refuse to pray. And I am Jonah every time I choose comfort over obedience.

Help me remember that while running from You might feel easy in the moment, it is always a downward journey.

Thank You for Your grace to wayward men and women through Jesus. Thank You for welcoming runaways back into Your arms. Help me follow You more fully.

Amen.

Discussion Questions

1. Before you picked up this book, how familiar were you with the story of Jonah?

2. Have you ever felt called by God to do something and wanted to run from that call? What happened?

3. Where is the last place you would want to be sent by God? Why?

4. What did you find surprising about the ancient Ninevites?

5. To what extent are you tempted to say no to things God has clearly said in His Word?

6. Have you ever struggled with God altering the trajectory of your life? What happened?

7. How do you respond to the quote from UK pastor Phil Moore, "It is much harder to say, 'yes' to God when we are successful"?

8. How might you be tempted to run from God in your own life?

Chapter 2: A Great Storm
(Jonah 1:4–16)

Then Yahweh hurled a great wind across the sea,
and a great storm developed on the sea,
and the ship threatened to break apart.
The sailors were fearful and each of them cried out to their god
as they hurled the cargo into the sea to lighten it.
But Jonah had gone down into the ship,
and lying down, he fell into a deep sleep.

Jonah 1:4–5

Did you ever run away from home as a child?

I never ran away from home (I had it too good!), but I did run away from school.

I was six or seven years old, and an older child came to our classroom with a note that said that I had to go and see the school principal, Mr. Cass. In those days, being called to the school office to see the principal was a scary thing, so even though I hadn't done anything wrong as far as I knew, I panicked.

So instead of following the path to the school office, I continued walking along the pathway straight out of school and down the road to our home.

My mother wasn't at home, so I let myself into the house, went down to my room, and started playing with my toys. It wasn't a bad way to spend a school day, and I soon forgot all about school—until there was a knock at the front door, and I heard the voice of the school receptionist calling my name. I crawled under the bed and hid there until my mother came home.

Then to my surprise, she took me back to school to face the music.

What we discovered as I sat in Mr. Cass's office and got severely scolded for running away from school, was that I was never meant to go and see him at all. The note was simply for me to come to the school office and pick up an envelope to take home to my parents.

And so the great irony of the story was that I ran away because I was afraid of seeing Mr. Cass ...

... and because I ran away, I did get to see Mr. Cass!

Often, when we ran away, we ended up hiding at a friend's house or going to the park down the road. And once we got tired or hungry or just bored, we packed up and went home again. Even if our runaway stories involved more drama than that, and we were a little bit older, most of the time, we look back on those moments in life with some embarrassment. We share our runaway stories sheepishly.

I wonder if that's how Jonah felt as he re-told his story of running away from God.[51]

When we left Jonah at the end of the last chapter, he had boarded a ship bound for the faraway city of Tarshish. He was running away from the clear command of Yahweh to go and preach in the great city of Nineveh.

And he may have thought that his decision to run from God was the end of the story.

But then verse 4 begins with a key phrase: "Then Yahweh …" The previous verse began with the words "but Jonah …" and now the next verse narrates the divine response "then Yahweh …"

Those simple opening words in verses 3 and 4 contain a profound theological idea.

God will never allow the rebellion and sin of His people to be the last word in their story.

Why? Because God is a God of grace.

He certainly allows us freedom to make choices in life, both good and bad. He gives us the freedom to run. And He may allow us to wander a long way over a long period. But because He is a loving and gracious Father, He will, at some point, reach out to pursue and discipline His wayward kids.

This is one of the key lessons of the opening chapter of Jonah.

Our sovereign and powerful God graciously and relentlessly pursues those who are truly His.

Whenever there is a "but Jonah …" there is always a "then Yahweh …"

For God's people, a "but Jonah …" is never the final word in the story.

This aspect of God's character is beautifully described in the New Testament book of Hebrews.

> Endure hardship as discipline; God is treating you as his children. For what children are not disciplined by their father? If

you are not disciplined—and everyone undergoes discipline—
then you are not legitimate, not true sons and daughters at
all. Moreover, we have all had human fathers who disciplined
us and we respected them for it. How much more should we
submit to the Father of spirits and live! They disciplined us for
a little while as they thought best; but God disciplines us for our
good, in order that we may share in his holiness. No discipline
seems pleasant at the time, but painful. Later on, however, it
produces a harvest of righteousness and peace for those who
have been trained by it. (Hebrews 12:7–11)

Notice that the writer says that the purpose of God's discipline in the
lives of His children is "that we may share in his holiness" (v.10). God
does not discipline His children to punish or be vindictive. Instead,
He is training and shaping us, with the goal of transforming us more
and more into His image.

As the writer to the Hebrews acknowledges, this doesn't mean that
discipline isn't painful.

It often can be.

But God disciplines and pursues and corrects out of a deep and
relentless love.

And as a loving heavenly Father, Yahweh begins to discipline His prophet.

The God of the Storm

Yahweh's discipline opens with Him sending a storm to stop Jonah in
his tracks. The language of verse 4 is incredibly graphic. It tells us that
Yahweh "hurled" a great wind onto the sea. That word is used twice
more in the chapter as the sailors hurled first the cargo into the sea
(verse 5) and later Jonah himself (verse 15).

It is a vivid and almost violent word that elsewhere in the Bible is used for hurling an object such as a spear.[52]

The image is of a great and powerful God who hurled a ferocious storm, like a baseball pitcher winding up and sending a thunderbolt across home base.

And what Yahweh sent was a "great" wind and a "great" storm. These are two more occurrences of this key term in the story that we have noted in the introduction. Yahweh had already described Nineveh as "the great city" (verse 2); now the narrator used the same word to picture the wind and storm that the Creator had sent.

And with the double use of this key word, we are meant to realize that this storm was unrelentingly powerful.

The storm was so great and powerful that the highly experienced sailors were terrified.

I was caught in a storm like that while crossing New Zealand's Cook Strait. The strait separates New Zealand's North and South Islands and is named after British explorer James Cook, who sailed through the strait in 1770.[53] It is one of the world's most notorious stretches of water with strong tidal flows that can result in very rough journeys between the islands on inter-island ferries.[54]

When I was around eleven, our family crossed Cook Strait one evening in the middle of a ferocious storm. We boarded in Wellington, the capital of New Zealand, at the foot of the North Island, and the ferry, which was a large vessel, was already rocking in its berth.

Once all the passengers were on board and vehicles were securely tied down, the ship set sail on its three-hour crossing.

Almost immediately, the captain's voice came over the speakers, welcoming everyone on board, before announcing that we would be enduring a *very* rough crossing that night. We were informed that all passengers needed to remain indoors rather than going out on the deck.

The boat was heaving and tossing even within the confines of Wellington's normally picturesque harbor, and we were barely out into the main part of the strait before I lost my last meal.

It was the worst storm I had ever been in.

But this great storm in Jonah 1 seemed to be multiple times worse. The storm was so violent that experienced sailors, men who had potentially spent their lives at sea, were terrified. Verse 5 almost suggests that they were panicking, crying to their respective gods in terror, and "hurling" (same word as verse 4) their valuable cargo overboard in a desperate attempt to lighten the ship.

> Death is just one wave away, and so they do everything they can to survive.[55]

And this is where we begin to note some of the satirical contrasts and ironies in this chapter. We have already noted in the introduction that satire and irony are key features of the narrative. And in this chapter, we see a number of tongue-in-cheek contrasts that are meant to make us smile.

Irony no. 1—The experienced sailors were terrified of the storm, but Jonah was asleep in the hold.

The contrast could not be starker.

Experienced mariners who had potentially been sailing the Mediterranean for decades and had probably faced an abundance of storms were terrified at the ferocity of this storm. And yet the inexperienced Jonah was so relaxed that he had gone down into the hold of the ship and fallen asleep.

Readers who are familiar with many of the stories of the Bible may well see here a fascinating comparison with the stories in the New Testament of Jesus sleeping during a storm on the Sea of Galilee.[56]

However, the contrast between Jesus and Jonah in these moments cannot be greater.[57]

Jesus was asleep, worn out from ministry, but perfectly content in the Father's will.

Jonah, on the other hand, was nowhere near doing God's will. He was running as fast as he could from what Yahweh had called him to do!

The second irony is then found in verse 6:

> The sea captain found him and said, "How can you be sleeping? Get up and call out to your god! Maybe your god will spare us a thought so that we will not perish."

There is no mention in the text, however, that Jonah ever prayed in the storm.

Irony no. 2—The pagan sailors desperately prayed to their gods, but Jonah refused to pray to the one true God.

The sailors in this story seemed to be from different nationalities and backgrounds, and each of them, in this moment of great fear and danger, cried out to their personal or national deity. None of those gods were real; none of them had the power to calm the storm. There is only one true God, Yahweh, whom Jonah would shortly describe as "the God of the heavens, who made the sea and the dry land" (verse 9).

But even though He is the all-powerful being who had hurled this wind and storm onto the sea, His prophet was the only person on the ship *not* praying.

Even when the captain of the ship begged Jonah to pray, Jonah refused.[58]

After all, it's hard to pray to the God you're running from.

The God of the Lots

The story intensified even more in verse 7. The desperate prayers of the sailors had not been answered; the attempt to lighten the ship by throwing the cargo overboard had made no difference.

So the sailors decided that someone on board must be responsible, and they agreed to cast lots to find out who it was.

Casting lots was used in multiple cultures in the ancient world as a way of discerning the will of the gods. For example, the Roman soldiers who crucified Jesus cast lots to see who would win His clothing.[59] The lots were pieces of stone, wood, or pottery on which the names of each person may have been written. The lot that was cast would show the name of the person who was chosen.[60]

Casting lots was also done numerous times by God's people in the Bible, including the high priest on the Day of Atonement,[61] Joshua in distributing the Promised Land among the tribes of Israel,[62] the priest Zechariah being chosen to burn incense in the temple,[63] and the apostles choosing the replacement for Judas Iscariot.[64]

The belief was that Yahweh would show His will or choice through the lot. Proverbs 16:33 reads, "The lot is cast into the lap, but its every decision is from the LORD [Yahweh]."

And that was what happened in the middle of this torrid storm on the Mediterranean Sea.

> The lot fell to Jonah. (Jonah 1:7b)

There is a simple brevity in that line.

Remember that the key idea of this chapter is that **our sovereign and powerful God graciously and relentlessly pursues those who are truly His.**

And that's what we see in this moment in the story—the sovereign and all-powerful God was pursuing His runaway prophet.

Jonah 1 reminds us that this sovereign God is so powerful that He can hurl a ferocious storm across the sea, yet also control the casting of tiny pieces of stone or pottery that unmasks His wayward prophet.

Yahweh was fully in control of the situation.

In response to the lot, the sailors peppered Jonah with a series of questions. They wanted to know who he was, where he was from, what he was doing, and most importantly, why the storm was threatening their lives.

The first question is perhaps the most important. Literally, it reads, "What have you done?" And in the original language, it is exactly the same question that Yahweh asked Adam in the Garden of Eden in Genesis 3. This exact question is asked five other times in the Hebrew scriptures,[65] and each time it "expresses moral outrage at what the speaker perceives as foolish behaviour."[66]

Brad Carr

Jonah's response in verse 9 forms the heart of this chapter[67] and introduces some more ironies in the story.

> He answered them, "I am a Hebrew and I fear Yahweh, the God of the heavens, who made the sea and the dry land" (Jonah 1:9).

Irony no. 3—Jonah had run from Yahweh because he wouldn't preach to pagans, but he ended up preaching to pagans.

One of the greatest ironies of this story is that the very thing that Jonah was trying to run away from—telling non-Israelites about the God of Israel—was the very thing he ended up doing.[68]

It seems from a careful reading of the book, that Jonah had a very cynical view of non-Israelites. Certainly, his prayer in chapter 2 would draw a strong contrast between himself and "those who keep clinging to their useless idols" (Jonah 2:8).

And yet in spite of himself, and despite being on the run from Yahweh, Jonah ended up standing on the heaving deck of a ship in the middle of a ferocious storm, telling unworthy pagan seamen about the one true God.

But there's an even sadder irony when you carefully read Jonah's words in verse 9.

Irony no. 4—Jonah claimed to fear Yahweh, to worship Almighty God, yet his actions showed he neither feared nor obeyed Yahweh.

The Old Testament often speaks about "the fear of Yahweh" (Proverbs 1:7). Generally, the term means to be in reverent awe of Yahweh as the one true God.[69] And that was how Jonah, almost proudly, described himself to the sailors—he was an Israelite who feared Yahweh.

But how can Jonah claim to fear Yahweh, to be in reverent awe of Him, when he was running away in complete disobedience to Yahweh's

34

command? Proverbs 14:2 says, "Whoever fears the LORD [Yahweh] walks uprightly, but those who despise Him are devious in their ways."

With a simple reading of that single proverb, Jonah seemed to be a person who despised Yahweh rather than one who feared Him.

The use of the word *fear* by Jonah sets up another amazing contrast with the pagan sailors. At the beginning of the chapter, when the storm was hurled by this sovereign God, the sailors "were fearful" of the storm (v. 5). However, in verse 10, when they heard who Jonah was and that he was fleeing from this all-powerful being, they were "greatly fearful."

Literally, they "feared a great fear." This is a Hebrew figure of speech that means they are *terrified*.

Their fear of the God of the storm was now greater than their fear of the storm itself.

That introduces another irony into the story.

Irony no. 5—The Israelite prophet claimed to fear Yahweh, but the pagan sailors ended up genuinely fearing Him.

Or as one commentator puts it, "Their great awe, then, contrasts with Jonah's rather small awe."[70]

Meanwhile, verse 11 reminds us that the storm was continuing to get worse. It had already been so ferocious that these experienced mariners were terrified, and now it seemed the storm was becoming even more severe.

So they asked Jonah how they could pacify his God and calm the sea, to which Jonah gave a surprising reply. "Pick me up and hurl me into the sea" (verse 12).

What is surprising about that response is that it was both drastic and unnecessary. It was ultimately what the sailors would be forced to do, as we will see shortly, because they had no other options.

But Jonah had options.

I am convinced that if Jonah had confessed his sin to Yahweh, repented of his decision to run away, and committed to obey the Word of Yahweh and go to Nineveh, the storm would have been calmed and Yahweh would have allowed them to turn around and head back to Joppa.[71] The whole point of the storm, after all, was to discipline Jonah and bring him to the point of repentance. Having done that, my belief is that Yahweh would have relented, and they would have sailed back in safety.

The problem is that Jonah didn't repent. And while he confessed his wrongdoing to the sailors in verse 12—"I know that it is on account of me that this great storm has come upon you"—he refused to confess that to Yahweh.

It appears that Jonah had a death wish—he would rather die than obey Yahweh and go and preach in Nineveh.

The God of the Calm

The sailors' response to Jonah's advice on how to calm the storm showed them to be people of character in the story. Rather than throw their unwanted guest overboard to his almost certain doom, they instead redoubled their efforts to row back to land (verse 13). But it was to no avail. No amount of effort was enough to overcome the power of the storm that was continuing to build and grow in its intensity.

But their best efforts on Jonah's behalf set up another irony.

Irony no. 6—The sailors showed great concern for Jonah's life, even though he had shown little concern for theirs.

While Jonah seemed to have a death wish, these unbelieving sailors were doing everything they could to safeguard his life. Even after hearing from this prophet how they could save their lives—by sacrificing his—they continued to try and protect him.

And once again, the contrast with Jonah was telling.

The only reason their lives were even at risk in this storm was Jonah's rebellion against God. They were innocent bystanders caught up in the consequences of Jonah's sin. And yet Jonah never seemed overly concerned that his actions had placed them in harm's way.

Finally, the moment arrived when the sailors accepted that they had run out of options. The storm was continuing to get worse (v. 11, 15), and there was nothing more to be done. Their passenger, the one to whom the lot had fallen, must be sacrificed to save the rest of them.

But what they did next, before throwing Jonah overboard, was stunning.

They prayed.

But they didn't pray to their impotent, useless gods who had proved to be powerless in the face of the storm. They now prayed to Yahweh, the God who had sent the storm. And once again, the irony is stunning.

Irony no. 7—While Jonah still refused to pray to Yahweh, the pagan sailors now cried out to Him.

Jonah was still speechless when it came to talking to the God he claimed to follow and fear, but these sailors were not. They now cried out to "Yahweh," specifically using the divine name that is used throughout the Old Testament to point to God's loving relationship with His people.

And the prayer that they prayed to Yahweh was one of confession. They knew that what they were about to do—throw Jonah overboard—was not right. But they were stuck. They had run out of options. And so they confessed their sin to Yahweh—something the wayward prophet was still unable or unwilling to do himself.

Irony no. 8—The sailors were quick to confess their wrongdoing to Yahweh, but Jonah still refused to confess his own sin.

The actions of the sailors towards the end of this narrative mirrored their actions at the beginning. When the scene opened with the great storm, the sailors were praying to their gods and hurling their valuable cargo overboard to save their lives. As the story ended, they were once again praying and hurling (it was the same verbs). Now, however, they were praying to Yahweh, the God of Jonah, and they were hurling Jonah himself overboard. But through Jonah's stubborn rebellion and Yahweh's relentless pursuit of him, they had been left with no other choice.

And from the way that verse 15 was written, the results seemed to have been almost instantaneous—"And the raging sea was still" (verse 15). "The moment Jonah went under the water, the storm switched off as suddenly as a light being turned off."[72]

The scene was once again reminiscent of the stories in the gospels where Jesus calmed the storms. And the response of the sailors was similar to Jesus's disciples many years later. "They were terrified and asked each other, 'Who is this? Even the wind and the waves obey him!'" (Mark 4:41).

The story concluded in verse 16 with an amazing response from the sailors.[73]

Jonah was now sinking beneath the waves (more on that in the next chapter). Meanwhile, these pagan sailors took another dramatic step towards the one true God, Yahweh.

Verse 16 repeated the statement of verse 10 that they literally "feared a great fear." But now the object of their great fear had moved from the storm to Yahweh, the God of the storm. The abject terror they had felt towards the storm had now morphed into a reverent awe of this God.

In the original Hebrew text, the final verse reads, "And the men *feared* a great *fear* of Yahweh, and they *sacrificed sacrifices* to Yahweh, and they *vowed vows*."

These two additional couplets suggested that these sailors had moved towards a saving faith in Yahweh.[74]

The language of sacrifices and vows comes directly from Israel's worship in the Old Testament. For example, Psalm 116:17–18 reads,

> I will sacrifice a thank-offering to you
>   and call on the name of the LORD [Yahweh].
> I will fulfil my vows to the LORD [Yahweh]
>   in the presence of all his people.

These sailors practiced all three elements of worship described in this psalm—they made sacrifices to Yahweh, they called on His name in prayer, and they made vows to Him. And what I believe that meant was that despite Jonah's best efforts to run from Yahweh and not be used to preach to non-Israelite pagans, these seamen had come to genuine faith in Yahweh.[75]

And that leads us to the final irony of the chapter.

Irony no. 9—*The sailors ended up coming to faith in Yahweh through Jonah, but the prophet wasn't there to see it.*

Instead, Jonah was sinking towards a watery grave, which we will hear about in the next chapter.

The God of the Story

When I teach seminars on how to study the Bible, one of the things I discuss when talking about the narratives of the Bible is how to recognize the key characters of a story. I teach people how to identify the *protagonist*, the primary character in the story, and the *antagonist*, who plays opposite them. I also point out that in the Bible, God is the additional divine character.

Sometimes He is in the center of the story in the spotlight; at other times, He is offstage yet still highly involved.

In Jonah chapter 1, Yahweh is on the stage and in the spotlight.

As we noted at the beginning of the chapter, Yahweh is not about to let Jonah's running away be the final word in the prophet's story. Instead, the "but Jonah ..." of verse 3 gives way to the "then Yahweh ..." of verse 4.

And what we find in the ensuing narrative is a God who is in control, a God who pursues, a God who disciplines.

Our sovereign and powerful God graciously and relentlessly pursues those who are truly His.

As a pastor, I have sat through the years with a wide variety of people who have been running from God.

I have sat with a husband whose affair has just been uncovered and who is unsure whether the hard work of repentance and reconciliation is worth it.

I have chatted with a young adult struggling with the faith she was raised in and the temptations of the world around her that she wants to experience.

I have talked with professionals sensing God's call into Christian ministry yet feeling the lure of the status and salary of the corporate world.

I have prayed for people who have drifted out of a dynamic faith until they have found themselves far away from their spiritual moorings.

Running from God can look utterly different in different people's lives. But one thing never changes—if we are truly God's children, He won't let us go. He may let us wander for a time. He might give us a lot of rope. But in the end, our wise and good Father will pursue us.

Powerfully.

Relentlessly.

Lovingly.

Because He loves us too much to let us go.[76]

I Am Jonah

So what do we learn about ourselves from this installment in Jonah's story?

Let me suggest four more ways in which we can be exactly like this wayward prophet.

1. I am Jonah when I assume I can run from God.

As we read Jonah's story and watch him attempt to run from God, it seemed as though the prophet assumed that he could disobey God and seek to run from His presence and rule, and that God wouldn't care. Yahweh would just let him go, and perhaps find another, more willing prophet to go to Nineveh.

But as we have seen from the rest of this chapter, God graciously and relentlessly pursues His children.

I am convinced that one of the lies of our enemy, the devil, is that we can sin and rebel against God and that it won't ultimately matter. He tries to reassure us that there won't be serious consequences for our rebellion.

Again, we see this in the story of the Fall of Adam and Eve at the beginning of the Bible in Genesis 3. Yahweh had already told our first parents that they could eat from any tree in the garden except one—the tree of the knowledge of good and evil. He warned Adam, "When you eat from it you will certainly die" (Genesis 2:17).

Yet in the next chapter, as the serpent entered the story, he deliberately contradicted God's warnings. "You will not certainly die … For God knows that when you eat from it your eyes will be opened, and you will be like God, knowing good and evil" (Genesis 3:4–5).

We have doubted God's warnings and downplayed the consequences of our sin ever since.

That was what Jonah seemed to do. He naively assumed that Yahweh would just let him go; that a holy God didn't care if His prophet, one of His people, didn't feel like obeying Him this time around.

But God does care.

There are consequences for sin.

And a gracious and powerful God *will* pursue His children.

One of the most powerful ways to resist temptation can be to stop and think through the consequences of our actions. Before we decide to try and run away from God, it will be wise to think about where that road might lead and what God might have to do to turn us around and bring us back.

I wonder if Jonah would have run if he could have seen the size of the storm and could have smelt the inside of the fish.

2. I am Jonah when I forget that my sin affects others' lives.

The sailors in chapter 1 were innocent bystanders in the story. They had nothing to do with Jonah's sin. They weren't cheering him on and encouraging him to disobey.

They simply got caught up in the storm that Jonah's sin had created.

Often, we can be fooled into thinking that if we give into temptation, if we choose to sin, it will only affect our lives. Our rebellion will be just between us and God.

But the fact is that sin is almost never simply a private issue in life. Sin will almost always bubble over into other people's lives and affect our relationships with others.

Especially the people we love.

I sat and talked with a young married couple who came to see me about their marriage. Outwardly, they seemed to have it all—a committed relationship, two lovely preschool children, stable careers, and a lovely home. Yet the outward image of a blissful marriage was a mirage that hid a painful brokenness.

Their struggle stemmed from the battle that the husband had fought for almost two decades with pornography. It had started in his teenage years and had quickly developed into an addiction. He had always presumed that the battle would disappear once he was married and enjoying sexual intimacy with his wife. Instead, what he discovered, to his horror, was that as time went on, his continued struggle with porn was actually undermining and destroying the intimacy of their marriage.

He was struggling with deep shame and self-loathing. She was overwhelmed with feelings of rejection and inadequacy because her husband desired other women. Their marriage was under severe threat.

Thankfully, with the guidance and help of a counsellor with training and experience in this area, their marriage survived and grew. But it was by no means an easy journey.

He thought it was just a private battle, a struggle that wouldn't affect anyone else.

But our sin always affects other people.

Our anger problems affect others.

Our bitterness affects others.

Our materialism affects others.

Our pride affects others.

Our racism affects others.

Our sin and rebellion against God will always affect the lives of other people around us, particularly those we love.

And like the sailors in Jonah 1, others get caught in the storms of our lives.

3. I am Jonah when my life doesn't measure up to what I say I believe.

Jonah's self-description in verse 9 haunts me:

> I am a Hebrew and I fear Yahweh, the God of the heavens, who made the sea and the dry land. (Jonah 1:9)

As we have seen, it is one of the great ironies of the story that Jonah could stand on the heaving deck in the middle of this storm that he had caused and still claim to fear God.

And yet how often are you and I the same?

How often have I claimed to be a follower of Jesus, and yet my life at that moment hasn't looked much like Jesus?

How often have I said I worship Him when my heart has been far from Him?

How often have I professed to fear Him but then been afraid to mention Him in conversations with others?

The smell of hypocrisy—of claiming one thing and yet living something else—often hangs over our lives.

That is why in the Sermon on the Mount, Jesus warned so strongly against practicing our faith so that others might notice:

> Be careful not to practice your righteousness in front of others *to be seen by them*. If you do, you will have no reward from your Father in heaven.
>
> So when you give to the needy, do not announce it with trumpets, as the hypocrites do in the synagogues and on the streets, *to be honoured by others* ...

> And when you pray, do not be like the hypocrites, for they love to pray standing in the synagogues and on the street corners *to be seen by others* ...

> When you fast, do not look somber as the hypocrites do, for they disfigure their faces *to show others they are fasting.* (Matthew 6:1-2, 5, 16)

Sadly, far too often, my life doesn't measure up to what I say I believe.

Just like Jonah.

4. I am Jonah when God saves others in spite of me, rather than because of me.

One of the high points of this wonderful book is seeing these pagan sailors come to saving faith in the God of the runaway prophet.

Ordinarily, this is what the prophets of Yahweh lived for—to see pagans, idolaters, and rebels, turn to the one true God in reverent fear and faith.

But not only did Jonah not realise these sailors had come to faith, as we already noted above, but he wasn't concerned about that. He hadn't been looking for an opportunity to speak about His God. He wasn't interested in conversation at all—he went straight for the bunks at the bottom of the ship.

He was not at all concerned about the eternal destiny of the other souls onboard.

And he only admitted who he was—and talked about the God that he served—when he was forced to.

One commentator described Jonah as the "anti-missionary"—the prophet who didn't want to proclaim.[77]

Unfortunately for Jonah, he served a "missionary God," who is intent on seeing people from all nations and languages and ethnicities come to faith in Him.

How often are we like Jonah?

How often do we fail to look for opportunities to speak about God?

How often do we fail to even see the doors that God has opened so that we might share our faith?

How often are we "anti-missionaries" trying to follow a missionary God?

God may still use us, just as He still used His wayward prophet. But how much better would it be if we were a willing and eager participant in the great missionary work of God in our world?

---

1. I am Jonah when I assume I can run from God.

2. I am Jonah when I forget that my sin affects others' lives.

3. I am Jonah when my life doesn't measure up to what I say I believe.

4. I am Jonah when God saves others in spite of me, rather than because of me.

Father,

I am Jonah.

The reality is that my life never really measures up to what I say I believe. Like Jonah, I can often claim to love You and to follow You, and yet so often, I can be running from You in big and small ways. I play around with sin and assume there won't be any consequences. I forget that my sinful choices and decisions can hurt others whom I love.

And because of my own sinfulness, I can easily become an "anti-missionary," failing to play my part in Your great missionary endeavor in this world.

Thank you that You are the God of relentless grace. Thank You that You love me in Christ so much that You pursue and discipline me. Thank You for Your commitment and passion to mold me into the image of Jesus.

Amen.

Discussion Questions

1. Did you ever run away from home (or school) as a child? Why did you run? What happened?

2. How do you respond to the idea in this chapter that God graciously and relentlessly pursues those who are truly His? Why?

3. The sailors got caught up in the storm because of Jonah's rebellion. How might our sinful choices affect other people's lives?

4. How might considering the potential consequences of sin help us resist temptation?

5. Why do you think Jonah responded to the storm so differently from experienced sailors?

6. To what extent does your life not measure up right now to what you say you believe?

7. How does Jonah 1 show God's sovereignty over His creation? How do you respond to that?

8. How does Jonah's story illustrate the futility of running from God?

Chapter 3: A Great Prayer
(Jonah 1:17–2:10)

And Jonah prayed to Yahweh his God from the depths of the fish, saying,
"I called out to Yahweh in my distress,
and He answered me.
From the depths of the grave I cried for help,
and You heard my cry."

Jonah 2:1–2

Gary Larson, the brilliant mind behind *The Far Side* cartoons and probably my favourite cartoonist, once produced an outstanding image of the story of Jonah.

A middle-aged Mrs. Jonah is standing at the open door to their home. Hands on hips, she cuts an indignant figure. Jonah, meanwhile, is leaning just outside the door, bedraggled, scruffy, unkempt, with a pool of water at his feet and a bemused look on his face. The caption of the cartoon are apparently Mrs. Jonah's words. "For crying out loud, Jonah! Three days late, covered with slime, and smelling like a fish! ... And what story have I got to swallow this time?"[78]

As I noted in the introduction to this book, many people today look at the story of Jonah, particularly the idea that he survived three days in the belly of a fish, as exactly that—a whale of a tale that is too extraordinary to be believed.

However, as I said earlier, the great fish is actually *not* a key feature of the story. The fish is only mentioned in three verses—Jonah 1:17, 2:1, and 2:10. And of course it's not a whale—at least not as far as the text is concerned. The species of fish is not stated—it is simply "a great fish."

The verses that mention the fish are really the frame around the main part of chapter 2—Jonah's prayer to Yahweh from inside the belly of the fish. Those three verses are the narrative parts of the story that showcase the prayer that makes up most of the chapter.

By the way, the chapter divisions in our Bibles are not part of the original text.[79] And while they often separate portions of God's Word in a way that is helpful, occasionally they are simply in the wrong place.[80] This is one of those places. While the rest of the chapter divisions in Jonah are indeed useful for separating the story, verse 17 of chapter 1 should really be the first verse of chapter 2. That's where it is positioned in the Hebrew Bible.[81]

So let's leave aside the great fish, and focus instead on the real heart of Jonah 2, his "great prayer."

As we jump into Jonah 2, we need to understand that there is some disagreement among scholars and ordinary readers about how to understand some key parts of the chapter.

For example, how should we understand Jonah's prayer to God from inside the fish?

Please or Thank You?

As we get started, let me ask you a question: what does Jonah pray inside the fish?

What is the focus of his prayer?

If you were to ask that question of anyone who was reasonably familiar with the story of Jonah, most people would respond that Jonah prayed for deliverance.

He pleaded for salvation.

As he lay inside the fish, Jonah cried out to God to rescue him.

Right?

Well, no, actually. That's not the case.

While most people assume that Jonah prayed a prayer asking for deliverance, that's not what we read in the text.[82]

Jonah's prayer was a prayer of thanks.

In fact, many scholars describe it as a *psalm* of thanksgiving, exactly what we find in the book of Psalms in the Old Testament. One commentator calls it, "a textbook example of a thanksgiving psalm."[83]

In other words, Jonah wasn't saying "please" to God.

He was saying, "thank you."

One of the ways we know this is that almost all the verbs in the psalm are in the past tense.[84] Jonah wasn't crying out to God to do something in the future—"save me!" He was celebrating something that God had already done in his past—"He has saved me." Notice the opening words of the psalm:

> I called out to Yahweh in my distress,
> and He answered me. (Jonah 2:2a)

At this moment in the story, Jonah had *already* called out to Yahweh, and Yahweh had *already* answered his request. Again, this psalm was not *asking* for God to deliver him; it was *celebrating* the deliverance that Jonah had already experienced.

By the way, this meant that Jonah had now prayed twice within a short period.[85] Having been completely reluctant to talk to Yahweh while on the ship (as we saw in the previous chapter), he had now cried out to God on two occasions—once for deliverance as he was drowning (as we shall see shortly), and now again as he lays inside the belly of the fish, reflecting on his salvation.

The first prayer in the sea was a "please."

The second prayer inside the fish was now a "thank you."

The other way we know this was a psalm of thanks is by the language that Jonah used.

He quoted numerous times from the book of Psalms, and he used the language from the psalms of thanksgiving. Perhaps the most obvious example would be Psalm 18, a song that David (the future king of Israel) wrote to thank God for rescuing him when he was being hunted by Israel's first king, Saul.

Compare verse 6 of that psalm to Jonah's opening words:

> In my distress I called to the LORD [Yahweh];
> I cried to my God for help. (Psalm 18:6)

> I called out to Yahweh in my distress,
> and he answered me. (Jonah 2:2a)

This psalm in Jonah chapter 2 uses the language and structure of the thanksgiving psalms as it remembers and celebrates what God has done.

This means that the fish wasn't the *problem* that Jonah needed to be rescued from.

The fish was the *rescuer.*

The fish was Jonah's *salvation.*

Yahweh sent the fish to rescue Jonah from drowning, and in response, Jonah prayed (or perhaps even sang) this psalm of thanksgiving.

Dead or Drowning?

A thanksgiving psalm generally has three components: an *opening declaration* of God's deliverance, a *poetic narrative* or description of what has happened, and a *closing vow* of thanks.[86]

That is what we find in this psalm.

We have already read Jonah's *opening declaration* of deliverance in verse 2. This opening declaration is expressed in third-person language—"He answered me"—while the rest of the psalm will use second-person language directly to God: "You heard my cry" (v. 2b).

From the second half of verse 2 through to verse 6, we then have Jonah's *poetic narrative* or description of what he was saved from.

Different commentators structure or summarize these verses in contrasting ways, but I have particularly appreciated the work of Kevin Youngblood. He suggests that there is a *chiasm* in verses 2b–6a with a second *chiasm* in the last section of the psalm from verses 6b – 9.[87]

A *chiasm* is the name given by scholars to a literary feature that is being increasingly recognized throughout the Old Testament. It takes its name from the Greek letter *chi,* which is shaped like the letter X.

In a chiasm, the outer sections at the beginning and end of a passage mirror each other, as do the next portions of the passage, until you reach the center.

According to Dr. Youngblood, the structure of the poetic narrative in Jonah 2 looks like this:

> **A** From the depths of the grave I cried for help,
>   and You heard my cry.
>
>> **B** You threw me into the depths,
>>   into the heart of the seas;
>>   the currents churned around me,
>>   all Your breakers and Your waves
>>   broke right over me.
>
>>> **C** I said, "I have been banished from Your sight;
>>>   but I will gaze once again to Your holy temple."
>
>> **B'** The waters surrounded me, threatening my very breath,
>>   the deep churned around me;
>>   seaweed wrapped around my head.
>
> **A'** To the bottom of the mountains I sank;
>   the seafloor barred me in forever.

What this structure helps us see is that the outer verses (verses 2b and 6) describe the depths to which Jonah sank after he was hurled from the ship. Verse 2b describes him crying out "from the depths of the grave," which is literally "the belly of Sheol."

Sheol was "a poetic term for the burial place of the dead, [so] Jonah sees his descent into the waters of the sea as bringing him to the brink of death."[88]

Verse 6 describes the same descent to the very depths of the sea, as though that is where the feet or the roots of the mountains can be found.

Now some have read these words through the years and assumed that Jonah actually died, either in the water or in the belly of the fish. And, taken literally, it can sound like that. He said he was deep in Sheol— the realm of the dead (v.2); he sank to the very roots of the mountains (v. 6a); and he was barred in forever (v. 6b).

If you then add that, in the gospels, Jesus Himself likened His death and resurrection to Jonah being in the fish for three days and nights (which we'll look at in chapter 7),[89] it can look as though Jonah might have literally died. One well-respected pastor once wrote,

> Years ago, I took the position, which I still hold today, that Jonah was not alive inside the fish but that he died and God raised him from the dead … My friend, don't you know that Jonah prayed his prayer the minute he went inside that fish? Then he lapsed, I'm sure, into unconsciousness and then death. And God raised him from the dead. He was dead inside the fish.[90]

However, my belief is that people who believe Jonah literally died have misread the poetic language.[91] Poetry in the Old Testament uses figurative and expressive language, just as a lot of modern poetry still does. Metaphors, hyperbole, personification, and other features are all part of poetic language, which means we need to work hard to understand exactly what the biblical author's meaning is in any figure of speech.[92]

As we read this prayer in Jonah 2, it helps to look at some of the other Old Testament psalms that Jonah drew his language from. For example, we have already noted the parallels between Jonah 2 and

Psalm 18. Here is what Psalm 18 says about calling out to Yahweh in distress (which comes right before the verse I have quoted earlier):

> The cords of death entangled me;
>> the torrents of destruction overwhelmed me.
> The cords of the grave coiled around me;
>> the snares of death confronted me. (Psalm 18:4–5)

Note again the similarity of language between Jonah 2 and Psalm 18.

Now I don't know anyone who believes, based on these verses in Psalm 18, that David literally died and was resurrected back to life when he was a fugitive. In fact, the narrative of 1 Samuel makes it clear again and again that Yahweh protected the life of his anointed future king.

David here was using poetic language to describe how close he came to death.

Jonah was doing the same thing.

Except in Jonah's case, the language of torrents and entanglements fitted his reality even better.

So Jonah didn't die. He just came close to death.

We see this in verses 3 and 5 in the next ring of verses (**B** and **B'** in the chiasm). They use the same graphic and poetic language as Psalm 18 to picture Jonah fighting for his life and almost drowning in the waves.

Listen again to the descriptions from these verses:

> Threw into the depths ...

> Currents churned ...

Breakers broke ...

Waters surrounded ...

The deep churned ...

Seaweed wrapped ...

It is as though Jonah wanted his readers to feel and imagine what it was like for him as he experienced the pounding of the waves, the engulfing currents, the panic of feeling like he was slipping away.

> This vivid description of Jonah's near-death experience serves as a dark backdrop against which the account of Yahweh's deliverance stands out in bold relief.[93]

All this dramatic language leads us to verse 4 in the center of the chiasm (represented by letter **C**), where Jonah expressed his desire to see Yahweh's holy temple. Again, this is Psalm 18 language, where the temple symbolizes the saving presence of Yahweh:

> From his temple he heard my voice;
>   my cry came before him, into his ears. (Psalm 18:6b)

This is where the first half of the prayer has been leading us—through the torrents and swirling water, the breakers and the seaweed, the choking and gasping for breath.

Jonah, the prophet who refused to pray in the opening chapter of the story, had finally cried out to his God.

And remarkably, Yahweh answered.

You may have thought at the end of chapter 1 that Jonah would disappear under the waves.

That we'd never hear from him again.

That it would be the end of the wayward, disobedient prophet.

But it wasn't.

Yahweh heard his cry from His holy temple.

This is a stunning reminder to us that we are never beyond the saving grace of God.

We can never run so far, we can never fall so deeply, we can never fail so often, that we are beyond crying out to God.

As we will see in the next chapter, He is the gracious God of second chances.

Humbled or Arrogant?

The language suddenly changes in the final part of verse 6, which introduces the last section of the psalm, a *closing vow* of thanks.

In this final section, Jonah beautifully *described his deliverance* (vv. 6b-7), made his *vow to praise* Yahweh again (vv. 8–9a), and ended his psalm with an *emphatic declaration* (v. 9b).

After the dramatic and graphic descriptions of Jonah's experience of near drowning, the final line of verse 6 announces a dramatic change in fortune:

> But You lifted up my life from the abyss,
>   Yahweh my God.

We noted in the last chapter that the "then Yahweh ..." statement in Jonah 1:4 was a key moment in the story and that whenever there is a "but Jonah ..." there is always a "then Yahweh ..."

Jonah himself acknowledged that as he celebrated the intervention of God in this psalm of thanksgiving. This is another "then Yahweh …" moment.

Once again, Jonah used the language of the thanksgiving psalms as he described being lifted from a pit.

Notice the similarities to the beginning of another thanksgiving psalm, Psalm 30:

> I will exalt you, LORD [Yahweh],
>> for you lifted me out of the depths
>> and did not let my enemies gloat over me.
> LORD [Yahweh] my God, I called to you for help,
>> and you healed me.
> You, LORD [Yahweh], brought me up from the realm of the dead;
>> you spared me from going down to the pit. (Psalm 30:1–3)

In verse 7, as his life was ebbing away (another word with connotations of the tides and sea),[94] Jonah said he "remembered Yahweh." This is a poetic way of describing prayer (Psalm 42:4, 6; 63:6). Almost at the last moment, it seemed, Jonah remembered Yahweh.

He prayed.

And he marveled that his prayer reached Yahweh's holy temple (verse 7b).

Like many thanksgiving psalms, Jonah's song then responded to this amazing deliverance that he had received. His response was a *vow to praise Yahweh*. Normally, this would involve sacrifices to Yahweh at the temple in Jerusalem, where after the sacrifice, the person who had been delivered would share their story with God's people and celebrate what God had done.

This was standard practice for a thanksgiving psalm.[95]

But notice the delicious irony of Jonah's vow. He said that his vow of praise would involve sacrifices and vows (verse 9), which, unbeknownst to him, was *exactly* how the pagan sailors on the ship had worshipped Yahweh at the end of chapter 1.

> The narrator … slyly intends his audience to draw a parallel between Jonah's experience and that of the seamen. Both faced a similar crisis, peril from the sea; both cried to Yahweh, acknowledging His sovereignty. Both were physically saved; both offered worship. Ironically Jonah is at last brought to the point the Gentile seamen have already reached.[96]

What are we to make of this language?

There is no doubt that Jonah had been humbled by his entire experience. This wayward prophet, who was intent on running from Yahweh's presence and almost seemed to have a death wish in chapter 1, had been brought to the place of humbling himself before God and crying out for rescue.

But while at one level Jonah had been humbled, I believe his own words betrayed his continued arrogance. Look at what he sang in verses 8–9:

> Those who keep clinging to their useless idols
>> spurn Your unfailing love.
> But as for me, with a song of thanks,
>> I will sacrifice to you;
>> what I have vowed I will fulfil. (Jonah 2:8-9)

Jonah here drew a very strong contrast between himself and "those who keep clinging to their useless idols."

There can be little doubt who he had in mind with the reference to those who worshipped false gods. Commentators are almost unanimous in their agreement that Jonah was clearly contrasting *his* faith in Yahweh with the pagan sailors he had left behind on the ship.[97]

He was very confident about his religious superiority over those pagans he had sailed with.

What he didn't know was that they had already offered a sacrifice to Yahweh (1:16).

They had also made vows.

They had come into a relationship with Jonah's God.

One commentator likens Jonah's arrogance in this story to the pride of the Pharisee in Jesus's parable in Luke 18:9–14.[98] Jesus described a Pharisee and a tax collector who went to pray at the temple, and while the tax collector humbled himself before God as a sinner, the Pharisee proudly assumed he was spiritually superior.

Ironically, at the end of His parable, Jesus said that only the tax collector went home justified before God.

> Those who compare themselves to others will always find reasons for pride; those who compare themselves to the Lord will realise their own wickedness, cry out humbly for His mercy and salvation, and then extend this mercy to others.[99]

While Jonah had definitely been humbled by his experience in the sea, it would soon become apparent that he continued to proudly assume he was better than pagans who he thought did not know Yahweh.

Brad Carr

Grateful or Unrepentant?

The psalm of Jonah ends on an emphatic note—a declaration of God's saving power:

> Salvation comes from Yahweh. (Jonah 2:9b)

This is "one of the most profoundly significant sayings"[100] in the Bible, and echoes yet another thanksgiving psalm—Psalm 3.

This is another psalm of David, this time from later in his life when he was on the run from his son Absalom, who was leading a coup against him as king (see 2 Samuel 15–18). The psalm is built around the idea of being delivered or saved, with David's enemies saying in verse 2, "God will not deliver him," which is followed by David's own prayer in verse 7. "Arise LORD [Yahweh]! Deliver me, my God!"

It is in this context that David then finished Psalm 3 with the emphatic statement,

> From the LORD [Yahweh] comes deliverance.
> May your blessing be on your people. (Psalm 3:8)

In other words, David finished his psalm with a confident declaration that Yahweh is the only God who saves.

Jonah finished his psalm on the same emphatic note.

The word we translate as "deliverance" or "salvation" is the Hebrew word *yeshua*, from which the biblical names of Joshua, Hosea, Isaiah, and Jesus are all derived.[101]

This is why in announcing Jesus's impending birth to Joseph in Matthew 1, the angel explained the baby's given name: "She will give birth to a son, and you are to give him the name *Jesus*, because he will *save* his people from their sins" (Matthew 1:21; emphasis mine).

Jonah, then, was echoing David's thanksgiving psalm in declaring that anyone who is saved owes God all the glory and praise for their deliverance, because salvation is God's domain.

> The prepositional phrase denotes possession. Salvation belongs to God alone, to no one else. If someone is saved, it is wholly God's doing. It is not a matter of God saving you partly and you saving yourself partly. No. God saves us. We do not and cannot save ourselves. That's the gospel.[102]

Jonah's closing line is therefore a profound theological statement about salvation.

It's also a statement of profound gratitude.

The chapter then closes with a single verse of narrative, that works with the opening verses (Jonah 1:17–2:1) to "frame" the psalm:

> Then Yahweh spoke to the fish and it vomited Jonah up onto the dry land. (Jonah 2:10)

As the first chapter of Jonah's story has already made abundantly clear, Yahweh was in complete control of the situation. Jonah 1:17 has already explained that when Jonah desperately cried out for salvation as he went beneath the waves, Yahweh "provided" a great fish. This verb will reappear in chapter 4, when Yahweh would "provide" a leafy plant, a hungry worm, and a scorching east wind (4:6–8) as He taught Jonah an important lesson.[103]

Now as the chapter comes to a close in Jonah 2:10, Yahweh spoke to the fish, and it vomited Jonah up onto the dry land, presumably somewhere along the coastline of Israel.

All this time Jonah has been in the fish travelling back to dry land. Now the journey is over. Yahweh speaks to the fish, his instrument of salvation for Jonah. It obediently and doubtless gladly spews up this indigestible object and swims off with a flick of its tail, is distinguished mission accomplished.[104]

Once again in this story, there is something deeply ironic about Jonah getting vomited onto the shore by the fish. Then and now, vomit is something with very negative connotations. It is often used through the Old Testament as a metaphor of judgment,[105] and suggests deep humiliation and ridicule. For example, the prophet Jeremiah declared,

> Make her drunk,
>> for she has defied the Lord [Yahweh].
> Let Moab wallow in her vomit;
>> let her be an object of ridicule. (Jeremiah 48:26)

Nonetheless, it was the last step of saving Jonah from his watery grave, and it sets up the next part of the story in chapter 3.

As we have seen, this prayer in Jonah 2 is profound, powerful, and incredibly biblical.

Jonah poured his heart out to Yahweh, incredibly grateful that despite his foolishness and sin, when he had sunk to the lowest point, Yahweh graciously heard his cry and responded with deliverance.

Yahweh didn't need to answer.

He didn't have to respond.

But He graciously chose to.

We can never run so far, we can never fall so deeply, we can never fail so often, that we are beyond crying out to God.

And Jonah was incredibly grateful.

However, there was something missing in this prayer.

You may not have noticed, but nowhere did Jonah admit that what he had done was wrong.

There was no confession of his sin.

There was no admission that he should not have run from Yahweh in the first place.

There was no repentance.

> Jonah's prayer is void of any acknowledgement of wrongdoing on his part. It is completely lacking in confession and penitence. His prayer acknowledges only that he was in danger; it never delves into the real reason for the circumstances from which he seeks deliverance.[106]

Old Testament professor Daniel Timmer makes an interesting observation in this regard. He notes that thanksgiving psalms could give thanks for Yahweh's deliverance from danger or give thanks for His salvation from sin. Both will be giving thanks for Yahweh's intervention. However, Timmer notes that when a psalmist is acknowledging personal sin and thanking Yahweh for salvation and forgiveness for sin, the confession of sin is a primary component of the psalm.

> Jonah, however, although he is unquestionably in dire straits because of his own disobedience, does not even recognise his own sin and so utters not a word of confession.[107]

In other words, Jonah was incredibly grateful to God for saving him from death.

But he was still not sorry for running from God in the first place.

I Am Jonah

So what do we learn from Jonah's thanksgiving psalm?

I have suggested that the key idea of this chapter is that **we can never run so far, we can never fall so deeply, we can never fail so often, that we are beyond crying out to God.**

Jonah is proof of that.

At the last possible moment, as he was descending into the sea and about to drown, he cried out to God.

And his thanksgiving psalm, composed in the belly of the great fish, testifies to his amazement that Yahweh actually heard his prayer and answered it.

We see this remarkable grace of God all through the Bible.

Back in chapter 1, I shared Tim Keller's suggestion that in the first two chapters of his story, Jonah looks remarkably like the younger of the two sons in Jesus's famous parable in Luke 15.[108] The younger boy, generally described as the prodigal, is the one who asks for his inheritance, leaves home, and heads to a far-off country where he loses everything.

Then at his lowest point, as he is feeding some pigs and sharing their supper, he decides to go home and throw himself on the mercy of his father. And his father extravagantly and graciously welcomes him home—running to embrace him, throwing a party, and publicly identifying him as his son once more.[109]

What a stunning picture of the grace of God.

It would certainly be appropriate to explore this amazing grace more at this point, but I will hold off and come back to this in the final chapter of this book, when we focus on the person of Jesus.

In the meantime, let's continue our reflections on Jonah and look at another four ways we can be exactly like this wayward prophet.

1. I am Jonah when my prayer life often revolves around moments of crises.

There is no escaping the reality of Jonah's prayer life.

Jonah had refused to pray in chapter 1—even when the captain pleaded with him or later when the pagan sailors began to cry out to his God. As we've already noted back in chapter 1, *I am Jonah when I fail to talk to God.*

However, it was as his life hit rock bottom, sinking beneath the waves, that suddenly he prayed.

As we have just noted, it is never too late to cry out to the God of all grace.

But the reality is that, just like Jonah, our prayer lives often languish until we're in deep trouble.

In the opening chapter of his superb book, *A Praying Life*, Paul Miller discusses a multitude of reasons why prayer is so difficult in our lives:

> Cynicism: "we don't think prayer makes much difference."

Distractions: "we last for fifteen seconds ... and our minds are off on a tangent."

Boredom: "we put together a prayer list ... but the list gets dull."

Busyness: "we are so busy that when we slow down to pray, we find it uncomfortable."

Restlessness: "we are uncomfortable with silence."

Self-reliance: "because we can do life without God, praying seems nice but unnecessary."[110]

Ouch! I don't know about you, but I find a list like that incredibly convicting.

Prayer has never been a strong part of my relationship with God. I have always had this nagging feeling that I'm a failure at prayer.

And yet I can read Jonah's story, and very quickly condemn him for his failure to pray until he was deep in the weeds.

Jonah's reason for not praying was quite different from the list above. Jonah failed to pray, not because he was distracted or busy or restless.

Jonah didn't pray because he was sinning.

In their book, *Praying*, J. I. Packer and Carolyn Nystrom quote nineteenth-century church leader J. C. Ryle.

Praying and sinning will never live together in the same heart. Prayer will consume sin, or sin will choke prayer. I cannot forget this.[111]

Ryle is right. When we carry unconfessed sin in our lives, our immediate tendency is to withdraw from God's presence. We instinctively sense our guilt when we try to pray. But that guilt is actually a prompt for us to go running back to the God of grace.

But regardless of the reason,

when we only pray occasionally,

when we're in trouble,

when we're at our wits end,

when we've got nowhere else to go,

we're being just like Jonah.

2. I am Jonah when I can quote the Bible but don't put it into practice.

It struck me as I was writing this chapter just how biblical Jonah was.

I don't mean that he was biblical in his behaviour; I'm talking about his knowledge of the scriptures.

I noted earlier that Jonah quoted numerous times from the book of Psalms. One author suggests that "a study of Jonah's prayer will show allusions or references to Psalms 3, 5, 16, 18, 31, 42, 50, 65, 88 and 120."[112]

But it was not like he had a library of scrolls with him inside the fish.

He must have known a lot of those psalms from memory.

All of which suggests that, as a good prophet of Yahweh, Jonah knew the scriptures.

The problem was, he didn't obey them.

He didn't put them into practice.

He didn't apply what he knew to his life.

One of my professors at seminary, Howard Hendricks, would often say, "The Bible was not written to satisfy your curiosity; it was written to transform your life."[113]

The New Testament book of James agrees.

> Do not merely listen to the word, and so deceive yourselves. *Do what it says* ... Whoever looks intently into the perfect law that gives freedom *and continues in it*—not forgetting what they have heard *but doing it*—they will be blessed in what they do. (James 1:22, 25; emphasis mine)

In his timeless classic, *Living by the Book*, Hendricks discusses four steps in applying the Bible to our lives.[114]

The first is to *know*.

We need to know *the Bible*. We often pit knowledge of the Bible against living it out. But they're not mutually exclusive. In fact, to apply the Bible, we have to know what it says.

Jonah's problem was that he didn't live out what he knew.

For many of us, the problem is that we don't know the Word well enough.

So we need to study the scriptures more, and then make sure we apply what we learn.

The other thing we need to know is *ourselves*. Hendricks quotes the apostle Paul's words to his young friend and associate Timothy:

Watch your life and doctrine closely. Persevere in them, because if you do, you will save both yourself and your hearers. (1 Timothy 4:16)

To apply the Bible to our lives, we need to have a correct and realistic understanding of ourselves. We need to be self-aware about our gifts, our struggles, our weak points, our strengths, and the areas where we're prone to temptation.

The better we know ourselves, the better we can apply God's Word to each area of our own lives.

By the way, this means we also need to be in a healthy community of other believers. For to truly know ourselves well, we need the input of others we trust.

In his wonderful book, *Leadership from the Inside Out*, Kevin Harney talks about the power of self-examination and knowing ourselves well.[115] He recalls having a skin cancer removed from his cheek in his thirties and the doctor stressing the importance of him continuing to keep a close eye on his skin. But the doctor has also told Kevin to have his wife, Sherry, check his back regularly. What Kevin then writes about leaders actually applies to all of us:

> Leaders need people who can help us identify potential areas of trouble we can't see. In a sense, we need people we love and respect to say, "I've got your back," and really mean it. We must have the courage to invite others to point out problems developing in our lives … Where we have blind spots, those who are close to us, can identify areas in which we need to repent, change, grow.[116]

The second step in applying the Bible to our lives according to Hendricks is to *relate*.

We must relate the Bible to life by thinking about what we're reading and how it might affect every part of life.

I teach a one-day seminar called *Feast* in churches on how to study the Bible. In the last session of the day, we talk about application, and I introduce them to a tool that I call the "application target." It has three concentric rings, much like an archer's target, that represent God, self, and others, with some suggested areas of application for the two outer rings.

I teach seminar participants to ask three simple questions from a Bible passage they are studying:

1. What does this passage teach me about **God** and what He is like?

2. What does this passage teach me about **myself** and the state of my soul?

3. What does this passage teach me about my relationships to **others**?

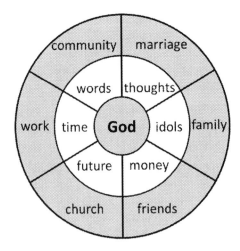

This simple tool has been especially helpful in thinking about how the truths of God's Word can relate to different aspects of life.

The third step is to *meditate*.

The Bible itself often calls us to meditate or ponder on God's Word as we go through each day.

> Be strong and very courageous. Be careful to obey all the law my servant Moses gave you; do not turn from it to the right or to the left, that you may be successful wherever you go. Keep this Book of the Law always on your lips; meditate on it day and night, so that you may be careful to do everything written in it. Then you will be prosperous and successful. (Joshua 1:7–8)

> Oh, how I love your law!
> I meditate on it all day long. (Psalm 119:97)

What does it mean to meditate on God's Word? During my childhood, when my dad would preach on the importance of meditating on God's Word, he would use the example of "barley sugars," a hard-boiled lolly or candy in New Zealand. Because they were so hard, it was never wise to try and bite down on a barley sugar. Instead, you would push it into the back corner of your cheek and suck on it, slowly allowing it to break down over time.

Dad would say that was what meditating on the Bible was all about. Take a single verse or concept from your reading or study of the Bible and just push it into the back corner of your mind. Through the day, just bring it to mind, ponder its truth in light of your own life, and allow the truths of God's Word to slowly dissolve into your mind and heart.[117]

Finally, Hendricks says that the fourth step is to *practice*.

Brad Carr

Ultimately, we need to respond to what God has said in His Word, and just do it! That's what James 1:22–25 is calling us to.

For knowing the Bible isn't enough. We need to apply it.

3. I am Jonah when I arrogantly look down on sinners instead of humbly reflecting God's grace.

One of the key reflections of this chapter is that even as Jonah was formulating a joyful, biblical psalm of thanksgiving to Yahweh, he continued to arrogantly assume his spiritual superiority over the pagan sailors.

The irony, as we noted earlier, is that the sailors had come to faith in Yahweh while Jonah was drowning and had already made their sacrifices and vows.

But just like the Pharisee in Jesus's parable in Luke 18, Jonah looked down his spiritual nose at people he felt did't measure up.

UK pastor Phil Moore suggests we can all be guilty of the same thing:

> His reaction reminds us that we can all develop no-go areas in our minds. If it isn't a particular ethnic group for you, it may be members of the gay or transgender community, or Muslims, or people much richer or poorer or older or younger than you are.[118]

The truth is that we can all be susceptible to a holier-than-thou attitude.

How do we change that? How can we develop and grow an attitude of gospel humility?

This is one of the apostle Paul's key concerns as he writes to his friends in the church at Philippi. He wrote to thank the church for their financial gifts and support (see Philippians 4:10–19) and to encourage them to stand firm as they faced opposition (see especially 1:27–30). But he was also concerned about a dispute between two key women in the church (4:2–3) and the need throughout the church for humility towards one another.

The way he encouraged humility, and an others-centered mindset, was by appealing to the sacrificial example of Jesus:

> Do nothing out of selfish ambition or vain conceit. Rather, in humility value others above yourselves, not looking to your own interests but each of you to the interests of the others.
>
> In your relationships with one another, have the same mindset as Christ Jesus:
>
> who, being in very nature God,
> did not consider equality with God something to be used to his own advantage;
> rather, he made himself nothing
> by taking the very nature of a servant,
> being made in human likeness.
> And being found in appearance as a man,
> he humbled himself
> by becoming obedient to death—
> even death on a cross! (Philippians 2:3–8)

In other words, the way to grow in gospel humility is by coming back to the cross of Jesus and reminding ourselves of the radical, self-giving love of Jesus.

The example of Jesus and the grace of God call us to humble ourselves in light of a love that we never deserved and can never repay.

> Jonah's own spiritual pride should have been humbled, of course, by the simple fact that he received what he did not

deserve: mercy instead of judgment, deliverance instead of death. This should have changed Jonah profoundly. It should change us profoundly. What our sin and rebellion earn is death (Romans 6:23). What God makes available to us in Jesus is life, an undeserved gift of his mercy and grace (Ephesians 2:1–9). This should destroy any spiritual pride we might have.[119]

4. I am Jonah when I fail to acknowledge the depth of my sin.

We noted at the end of our journey through Jonah's prayer, that while the psalm was beautiful and biblical, and Jonah was obviously grateful and thankful, there was a glaring omission.

Jonah never confessed his sin.

There was no remorse.

There was no genuine repentance.

While he was thankful for being delivered from a watery grave, I am not convinced that Jonah fully acknowledged the depth of his sin.

The problem is that I'm not sure that I do either.

Dr. D. A. Carson has noted that while the twentieth century was easily the bloodiest and most damaging in human history,

> Many in our generation have come to think of themselves as essentially good people. Pollyannaish outlooks abound … Doubtless every generation thinks of itself as better than it actually is, but in the Western world this generation has multiplied such moral blindness to the highest degree.[120]

This minimization of sin in our wider culture has affected us within the church more than we realize. What is true in the wider culture—and I think Dr Carson has it absolutely right—is also true within the church.

We tend to minimize sin, particularly in our own lives.

In his insightful book entitled *Respectable Sins*, Jerry Bridges suggests that "we, like society at large, live in denial of our sin."[121] He comments further:

> Our gossip or unkind words about a brother or sister in Christ roll easily off our tongues without any awareness of wrongdoing. We harbour hurts over wrongs long past without any effort to forgive as God has forgiven us. We look down our religious noses at "sinners" in society without any sense of a humble "there but for the grace of God go I" spirit …
>
> Why do we not also mourn over our selfishness, our critical spirit, our impatience, and our anger?[122]

Why indeed?

---

1. I am Jonah when my prayer life often revolves around moments of crises.

2. I am Jonah when I can quote the Bible but don't put it into practice.

3. I am Jonah when I arrogantly look down on sinners instead of humbly reflecting God's grace.

4. I am Jonah when I fail to acknowledge the depth of my sin.

Brad Carr

Father,

I am Jonah.

I so often only come running to You when I'm in trouble or when my life is falling apart. Like Jonah, I can put on such a spiritual front and show off my knowledge of the Bible, but I struggle to walk consistently and prayerfully with You. I long to be more consistent, more prayerful.

Lord, I am challenged too by the arrogance and pride that I see in Jonah but also in me. I seem to be able to identify sin in other people's lives so much more quickly than my own. I confess that I am guilty of harboring and practicing "respectable sins" in my own life, while looking down my nose at others. I seem to be able to justify my sinful choices much more than simply confess them to You.

Lord, help me reflect more on the wonder of the cross and the beauty of grace. Help me remember that I have no cause for pride. Please help me appreciate the depth of my sin, but even more, the vastness of Your forgiveness and grace in Jesus.

Amen.

Discussion Questions

1. Jonah 2 records Jonah's first prayer to God in the story. Do you think a lack of prayer in our lives can be an accurate gauge of where our relationship with God is at? Why or why not?

2. This chapter suggests that the fish is the rescuer of Jonah rather than God's tool of judgment. How does that change the way we might understand Jonah's prayer?

3. Jonah's psalm of thanksgiving was written from the belly of a fish. How is it possible to praise and thank God when we are still facing difficult or horrible situations?

4. In the middle of his psalm, Jonah recorded that God heard His prayer. Why is that surprising to Jonah? What does it teach us about God?

5. Why do you think our prayer lives so often improve when we are in a crisis?

6. Like Jonah, there's often a gap in our lives between what we know of the Bible and what we live out. How can we close that gap and ensure we apply the Bible more in our lives?

7. To what extent are you tempted to look down on others who may not have it as together as you do?

8. How do you respond to this comment from Jerry Bridges: "We, like society at large, live in denial of our sin"? Explain.

Chapter 4: A Great City
(Jonah 3:1–10)

Then the word of Yahweh came to Jonah the second time, saying:
"Get up and go to the great city of Nineveh and proclaim to it
the proclamation I will give to you."
So Jonah got up and went to Nineveh in
obedience to the word of Yahweh.

Jonah 3:1–3a

Imagine you're in business, and you have the opportunity to sign the biggest client you have ever had. This account will transform your bottom line and set your business up for years to come. And so you decide to assign the account to the salesperson who has lost a major client a few weeks before.

Or imagine you're a sports coach, and your team is playing in the grand final. It's the last quarter, and your team is down by two points with one minute to play. And you decide to pull your star playmaker from the field and replace them with the player who has lost the ball earlier in the season, and who's been warming the bench ever since.

Or imagine you're in charge of the production at the school or theater company. And after all the casting and call-backs are completed, you decide to give the starring role to the child who has gotten stage fright and run out of the theater in tears in last year's performance.

Or imagine you're the chair of the surgical department at the local hospital. A patient has arrived, needing a complex and dangerous procedure on their heart. It carries significant risk of death if something goes wrong. And you decide to roster the youngest and most inexperienced team member for the surgery, who has just lost a patient earlier in the week during a much simpler operation.

It just won't happen, will it?

That's not how our world works.

You don't give the failed salesperson the most important potential client.

You don't call on the player who has lost the ball when the game is on the line.

You don't cast the anxious child who suffers from stage fright as the lead role.

You don't roster the bumbling surgeon for the most complex procedure of the year.

You don't give the important tasks to the people who have blown it.

You don't put your trust in a failure.

At best, what happens with someone who has messed up spectacularly, is they may be given small opportunities to rebuild their confidence. We may choose to give them less significant tasks to see if they can cope. They may be given the chance to try again.

Or they may not.

What we definitely don't do is immediately entrust them with something big again.

And in many ways, that's biblical.

Jesus Himself talked about those who have been faithful with a few things being trusted with more.[123] On another occasion, He said,

> Whoever can be trusted with very little can also be trusted with much, and whoever is dishonest with very little will also be dishonest with much. (Luke 16:10)

When Paul wrote to an associate about who to appoint to church leadership roles, he wrote,

> They must first be tested; and then if there is nothing against them, let them serve as deacons. (1 Timothy 3:10)

In other words, it is biblical wisdom to only trust significant things to people who have shown they can be trusted.

But then the Bible has story after story of God doing the exact opposite. Moses tried to lead a failed revolution, and after forty years of pondering his failure, God called him to lead the Exodus from Egypt.[124] Peter was reinstated to his leadership role among Jesus's disciples after spectacularly denying that he ever knew Him.[125] Paul was trusted with God's mission to the Gentile world after hunting down the early followers of "The Way."[126]

Why?

Because our gracious God is the God of the second chance.

> He specializes in second chances. When we've messed up. When we've rebelled. When we've recoiled at the plans He's unfolded before us, we still get another chance.[127]

For that's who God is.

God is the kind of God who passes the ball to the player who has lost it.

God is the kind of God who gives the major client to the salesperson who has lost the last account.

God is the kind of God who gives the starring role to a frightened child or hands the scalpel to the inexperienced doctor.

Now this is where the metaphor can break down because I'm not trying to suggest that God is irresponsible. I am simply pointing out that numerous times in the Bible, God goes against what we will consider to be conventional wisdom and uses people who have failed.

Why? Because God is the kind of God who calls a runaway prophet *a second time* to complete the task he has been given.

That's what we find as we come to Jonah chapter 3.

Yahweh Surprisingly Forgives and Calls

Jonah 3 revolves around four surprising actions.

The first is in the opening two verses of the chapter, where Yahweh commanded Jonah to go to Nineveh a second time. In fact, the wording of these three verses deliberately echoes the opening three verses of the story in chapter 1. Look at the comparison between Jonah 1:1 and 3:1.

> Now the word of Yahweh came to Jonah son of Amittai, saying ... (Jonah 1:1)

> Then the word of Yahweh came to Jonah the second time, saying ... (Jonah 3:1)

Apart from the final words, "a second time," the opening verses in the original Hebrew text are exactly the same.[128] This contributes to the symmetry between the two halves of the book that we have discussed in the introduction.[129]

This repetition also powerfully portrays the grace of God.

Yahweh is not put off by Jonah's disobedience.

Yahweh's plan is not abandoned because of Jonah's failure.

Yahweh doesn't discard the failed prophet and look for someone else.

Instead, "the word of Yahweh came to Jonah the second time."

Why? **Because our gracious God is the God of the second chance.**[130]

Now Yahweh *doesn't have to* be gracious. He *doesn't have to* show grace. He *doesn't have to* offer a second chance to this rebel. And there are times in the biblical story when God chooses in His sovereignty *not* to offer a second chance.

When Moses disobeyed God during the wilderness wanderings, he lost the chance to enter the Promised Land.[131]

When King Uzziah pridefully usurped the exclusive role of the priests in the temple, he was struck with leprosy.[132]

When Ananias and Sapphira lied to the early church leaders about how much money their property had sold for, they fell down dead.[133]

These stories remind us that we cannot assume God's graciousness. We can't willfully and deliberately sin against God, expecting Him to be automatically gracious and forgiving. Sometimes, as we've already seen, God chooses to discipline His children.

Sometimes God allows us to reap what we have sown.[134]

But God's nature *is* gracious and forgiving.[135]

At His core, He is a God of grace.

He is the God of the second chance.

When we come to verse 2, there is a subtle but important change in the wording compared with the opening chapter of the story. When Yahweh first called Jonah in chapter 1, He said,

> Get up and go to the great city of Nineveh and *proclaim against it*, because their evil has risen up to me. (Jonah 1:2; emphasis mine)

However, in chapter 3, Yahweh commanded,

> Get up and go to the great city of Nineveh and *proclaim to it* the proclamation I will give to you. (Jonah 3:2; emphasis mine)

Once again, the first part of the verse is the same as Yahweh commanded His prophet to arise and go to the great city of Nineveh. And as my translation makes clear, the task remains the same, to "proclaim" or "preach" a message to the inhabitants of the city (even though the NIV translates the Hebrew word differently in the two chapters).

The difference, however, is found in the prepositions that convey the *purpose* of the proclamation. In chapter 1, Jonah was commanded to preach *against* Nineveh, suggesting a tone of judgment and condemnation for their sin. In chapter 3, on the other hand, he was commanded to preach *to* the city, which suggests a different posture.[136]

This may be an indication that Yahweh was willing to be gracious to the Ninevites despite the great sin of the city.

This could be a suggestion that the same grace that had been shown to the prophet of Israel who ran away was also available to this great pagan city despite its wickedness.

But this may also be a reminder to Jonah himself that Yahweh is not only a God of judgment, but also a God who delights in the repentance and turning of sinful people.

Jonah Surprisingly Obeys and Preaches

This leads us to the second great surprise of the chapter. At the beginning of the book, when the call of Yahweh had come to His prophet, Jonah had fled. In chapter 1, we read:

> But Jonah got up and ran away to Tarshish, far away from Yahweh. (Jonah 1:3)

However, Jonah's actions were diametrically different in chapter 3:

> So Jonah got up and went to Nineveh in obedience to the word of Yahweh. (Jonah 3:3)

For those who are familiar with the story of Jonah, this is no surprise at all. We knew this was coming. But for those who aren't familiar with it or are reading or hearing the story for the first time, this will be a surprise.

The expectation would be that if Jonah had run once, he could do it again.

But he didn't.

Surprisingly, Jonah heard the word of Yahweh—and obeyed.

He didn't run out the door.

He didn't call the travel agent.

He didn't head for Joppa.

He obeyed and went to Nineveh.

We need to give Jonah credit here. In chapter 1, we talked about how despicable and cruel the Ninevites were. I tried to highlight the brutality and horror of the Assyrian Empire.

They were the Nazis of the ancient world, the original terrorist state.[137]

And to his credit, despite the danger, Jonah obeyed the word of Yahweh and walked into the city of his enemies.

And what a city it was!

Just before we're told about Jonah's ministry in Nineveh, we are given one more reminder about how large the city is. It's already been described as "the great city of Nineveh" in Jonah 1:2 and 3:2 when Yahweh commanded Jonah to preach there. Now in Jonah 3:3 there as in additional comment:

> Now Nineveh was a great city to God; and it took a three-day journey.

There have been various ways in which the reference to walking through Nineveh in three days has been understood. Some read that as hyperbole since the ancient city, as large as it was for the time, would not have required that long to walk through it. Others suggest that the description includes the pasture lands and outlying towns that were part of the overall metropolis.

Perhaps the most convincing [explanation] is that it required three days to proclaim the message in all the public squares. It would take three days to walk and preach in every neighborhood and to complete the proclamation to everyone in the city.[138]

The most interesting part of this description of Nineveh, however, is the additional comment made in verse 3. In both Jonah 1:2 and 3:2, when Yahweh commanded Jonah to go to the city, it is described as "the great city of Nineveh."

In this editorial comment about its size, however, it adds an extra word. "Nineveh was a great city *to God*" (emphasis mine). The additional word is *elohim*, usually translated as "God" or "the gods" (depending on the context).

Now that can be a Hebraic way of saying "very," which is the way the NIV translates the sentence: "Now Nineveh was a *very* large city" (emphasis mine). Translating it as an idiom is certainly an acceptable translation of the original text.[139]

It can also be translated, "Nineveh was a great city *to the gods*" as a reference to the false gods of the Assyrians.[140]

However, the best translation is probably the most literal, which I have used. "Nineveh was a great city *to God*."[141]

In other words, it isn't just a large or important city geographically, politically, or economically.

It is an important city to Yahweh, the God of Israel. Despite its great evil, despite its terrorizing of the ancient world, despite its boasting and its wickedness—Yahweh loved the city of Nineveh.

God loved it enough to send—and then send again—a rebellious prophet.

And God loved it enough, centuries later, to send His one and only Son.[142]

Once he arrived in Nineveh, Jonah began to preach. The record of his message is found in verse 4:

> Forty days and then Nineveh will be overthrown!

In my translation in English, it's a total of eight words; in the original Hebrew text, it's only five.[143]

There are differences of opinion among commentators over whether this is simply a summary of what Jonah said, or whether this was *all* that he preached. In other words, did Jonah say a great deal in his preaching about the coming judgment of the Ninevites, and the narrator had just recorded the summary version for us? Or did Jonah walk from one street corner to the next over multiple days, repeating the same five-word phrase?

Either way, what is clear is that what Jonah preached is condemnation.

Whether these were the only words he pronounced, or whether this was the shorthand version of a longer message, there were some significant things missing in Jonah's message.

There was no statement about the God who had sent Jonah with this message.

There were no reasons given for why judgment was coming on Nineveh, so people would understand what they had done wrong.[144]

And most importantly, there was no explanation about how the people could escape this impending judgment.

There was no message about deliverance.

There was no mention of a second chance.

There was no word of grace.

There was simply a stark message of seemingly inevitable judgment.

It reads as though Jonah preached what previous generations of church-goers would call a "fire and brimstone" message.

And I mean that quite literally.

The key word in the summary of Jonah's message is *overthrown*. This word (*hapak*) means to be overturned or annihilated.[145] Its most famous use is in the Old Testament story of the destruction of the cities of Sodom and Gomorrah in Genesis 19, when God rained down burning sulfur in divine judgment of their wickedness.

> Then the LORD [Yahweh] rained down burning sulfur on Sodom and Gomorrah—from the LORD [Yahweh] out of the heavens. Thus he overthrew [*hapak*] those cities and the entire plain, destroying all those living in the cities. (Genesis 19:24–25)

So Jewish readers of Jonah's story would have immediately understood the kind of judgment that Jonah was preaching in Nineveh, even if the inhabitants of the city did not.

Yahweh was threatening to do to the city of Nineveh what He had done to Sodom and Gomorrah.

And it seemed as though that was pretty much all that Jonah announced.

That leaves us with a very interesting portrait of Jonah.

He was not the runaway prophet anymore—he obeyed the word of Yahweh and went to Nineveh as he was told.

But it feels like he was there under compulsion.

He announced the message of Yahweh's judgment, but he did not tell them about Yahweh's grace.

He was not about to let them know that he served the God of second chances.

That means Jonah was still a reluctant prophet.

The Ninevites Surprisingly Hear and Respond

The third surprise of the chapter, however, is that despite Jonah's reticence, the people of Nineveh responded.

It seemed as though they were given no word of hope, no message of grace, no explanation of how to repent and escape this impending judgment.

But the people repented anyway.

And what is most remarkable is that it was *all of them*.

Every

Last

One.

From the greatest of them down to the least. (Jonah 3:5)

The entire city of Nineveh, including its king, repented (verses 6–9).

But what exactly does that mean?

Almost all commentators believe that the inhabitants of Nineveh genuinely repented from their violent and sinful ways. This means they turned from their sin.

However, most commentators *don't* believe that means the Ninevites became followers of Yahweh. To use New Testament language, they were not born again.[146]

For example, you will have worked out by now that Tim Keller is one of my favorite authors both on Jonah and on the rest of the Bible. On this topic, he writes,

> We must not be too quick to liken Nineveh's "turning" to the revivals of modern church history. While it says they "believed God" (verse 5), there is no indication that the Ninevites came into a covenant relationship with the God of Israel ... That is why almost all commentators agree that Jonah did not successfully convert the Ninevites.[147]

In support of this claim, Keller points out that the Ninevites never used the personal, covenant name *Yahweh* (instead using the generic title *Elohim* or God). He also references the fact that there was no mention of forsaking their gods, offering sacrifices, or practicing circumcision.[148]

As much as I deeply respect Keller, however, I am in the small group of people who disagree with that assessment.[149]

I believe the Ninevites came to faith in Yahweh.

Genuine, saving faith.

Let me suggest five reasons why.

1. They Believe God

First, notice carefully the opening words of verse 5: *"The Ninevites believed God."* Keller notes these words from verse 5 in his quote above, but he doesn't seem to consider the ramifications of those words.

And I believe they are huge!

One commentator, Rosemary Nixon, goes so far as to suggest "This phrase is the turning point of the book."[150]

She makes that claim because verse 5 uses the same terms as one of the most theologically important phrases in the entire Old Testament:

> Abram *believed* the LORD [Yahweh], and he credited it to him as righteousness. (Genesis 15:6; emphasis mine)

Throughout the New Testament, Abraham (which is what his name Abram was changed to in Genesis 17) was held up as the model of saving faith. The apostle Paul quoted Genesis 15:6 in his letters to both the Romans and the Galatians as part of his argument that we are saved by faith alone and not by our works.[151]

And the same phrase is used of the people of Nineveh in their response to Yahweh.

Notice that the text doesn't say that the people of Nineveh believed *Jonah.*

It says they believed *God.*

In other words, this is not just a statement about them taking the message they heard seriously. It means they chose to trust in and believe the One who had sent the messenger.

In fact, one commentator even translates the phrase as, "they trusted God."[152]

> The verb that describes the audience's response to Jonah, "they trusted God" recalls the exemplary faith of Abraham, who similarly "believed God," with the result that Yahweh regarded him as just (Gen. 15:6). The idiom conveys a trust that relies on what another has said and leads the one trusting to act accordingly ... While the text does not go so far as to say that the citizens of Nineveh converted to the monotheistic worship of Yahweh, it certainly points in the direction of the Gentiles inclusion in God's covenant.[153]

Several commentators have pointed out that the key difference between Abram's faith in Genesis 15 and the response of the Ninevites in Jonah 3:5 is that Abram believed *Yahweh*, while the Ninevites only believed in *God (Elohim)*.

This is one of the key reasons that Keller does not believe that the Ninevites came to saving faith.

In fact, it is often also pointed out that this is different from the pagan sailors in chapter 1 of Jonah, who, we are told clearly in the text, came to faith in *Yahweh* (Jonah 1:14–16).

What is often overlooked, however, is that Jonah had explicitly told the sailors in chapter 1 that he served "Yahweh, the God of the heavens" (Jonah 1:9). Jonah had introduced the sailors to God's covenant name, Yahweh. Therefore, when they saw the storm become completely calm and believed in the God whom Jonah had told them about, they believed in Yahweh.

They had been told that *Yahweh* was the name of the one true God.

However, that does not seem to be the case in chapter 3. As we have already seen, Jonah seemed to preach little more than a stark message of judgment. He seemed to go out of his way to *not* tell the people of Nineveh about Yahweh.

It therefore seems quite harsh to say that the Ninevites' faith and trust in God was not genuine because they had not been told the divine name.

The fact is that the Ninevites responded to the revelation they had received about the character and intentions of God, and their response—like Abraham centuries before—was one of trust.[154]

2. They Show Repentance through Their Actions

The second reason I believe that they had a genuine, saving faith in Yahweh is their actions. Their belief in Yahweh's message resulted in a dramatic response.

This was exemplified by the actions of the king in verse 6.

> When the message reached the king of Nineveh, he got up from his throne, removed his robes, covered himself with sackcloth and sat down in the ashes. (Jonah 3:6).

Notice the progression of the king's actions that form another small chiasm:

> **A** He got up from his throne
> > **B** Removed his robes
> > **B'** Covered himself with sackcloth
> **A'** And sat down in the ashes

The outer lines (**A** and **A'**) show the change in *where the king was sitting*—he moved from his throne to sit in the ashes or dust as a sign of humility.

The inner two lines (**B** and **B'**) talk about *what he wore*. He changed out of his robes and put on sackcloth. Not only that, but the king also ordered the entire city, even the animals, to put on sackcloth, and declared a city-wide fast.[155]

This is remarkable, particularly when we remember that Jonah didn't seem to have told the people of Nineveh anything about how to respond to this message of judgment or how to approach Yahweh in contrition or repentance.

Just as the faith of the sailors in chapter 1 can be seen in their actions of offering sacrifices and making vows to Yahweh (Jonah 1:16), so I believe that we should see these actions of fasting and sackcloth as indications of the genuine repentance and faith of the Ninevites.

Their actions were amazingly scriptural.

> Put on sackcloth, you priests, and mourn;
>> wail, you who minister before the altar.
> Come, spend the night in sackcloth,
>> you who minister before my God …
>
> Declare a holy fast;
>> call a sacred assembly. (Joel 1:13–14)

Obviously, Joel 1 was addressed to the priests of Israel who ministered before Yahweh's altar, rather than the king and people of Nineveh. They were not even part of the covenant people of Israel.

Yet should we assume that Yahweh's words would not apply to foreigners who fulfilled these actions? Are we to believe that Yahweh would not hear their cry, see the actions of these people, and respond as He promised He would do in Joel?

> "Even now," declares the LORD [Yahweh],
>> "return to me with all your heart,
>> with fasting and weeping and mourning."

> Rend your heart
>> and not your garments.
> Return to the LORD [Yahweh] your God,
>> for he is gracious and compassionate,
> slow to anger and abounding in love,
>> and he relents from sending calamity.
> Who knows? He may turn and relent
>> and leave behind a blessing—
> grain offerings and drink offerings
>> for the LORD [Yahweh] your God. (Joel 2:12–14)

Don't miss the echo of Joel 2:14 in the closing words of the king of Nineveh:

> Who knows? God may change His mind and relent and withdraw his burning anger so that we might not perish. (Jonah 3:9)[156]

3. They Turn from Their Sin

Third, in addition to ordering putting on sackcloth and fasting, the king also commanded the people to call on God and turn from their evil and violence (Jonah 3:8).

The command to "cry out earnestly to God" (verse 8) is virtually the same words as the request of the captain to Jonah when he was asleep in the ship's hold in chapter 1, to pray to his God.[157]

> This verbal correlation emphasizes the parallel roles that each of these characters plays. Each is the leader of his community, and each one issues a command to pray.[158]

And not only did the king command the people to pray to God, which was a *positive* action, but he also told them *negatively* to turn from their sin. This is hugely significant in light of all that we have learned about the barbaric practices of the Assyrians. But this is a call to what the Bible describes as repentance—a change of mind resulting in a change of action.

> The king states that the people's outward signs of repentance must be matched by their turning from their evil ways and the wrong they have done. The king realizes that outward signs of repentance—like fasting or sackcloth or prayer—are useless if not accompanied by a change of life (v.8; cf. Isa. 58:3-9).[159]

Once again, this is in keeping with what the prophets constantly called for in the Old Testament:

> Seek the LORD [Yahweh] while he may be found;
>   call on him while he is near.
> Let the wicked forsake their ways
>   and the unrighteous their thoughts.
> Let them turn to the LORD [Yahweh], and he will have mercy on them,
>   to our God, for he will freely pardon. (Isaiah 55:6–7)

And don't miss the fact that verse 10 tells us that Yahweh saw that the people had turned from their sin. The God who sees the human heart saw that the people of Nineveh had genuinely repented of their sin.

4. Their Actions Mirror the Sailors

The fourth reason I think this is genuine faith is that, as we look at the structure of the book of Jonah as a whole and the mirroring of the two halves of the book, it makes sense to assume that both the pagan sailors in chapter 1 and the pagan citizens in chapter 3 came to faith through the reluctant prophet.

This is the way that the structure of the narrative works.

Look again at the structure of the book that I have presented in the introduction:

Section One	Section Two
Jonah 1—A Great Storm	**Jonah 3—A Great City**
God calls.	God calls (again).
Jonah runs.	Jonah obeys.
God pursues and saves.	God pursues and saves.
Pagan sailors believe.	Pagan Ninevites believe.
Jonah 2—A Great Prayer	**Jonah 4—A Great Lesson**
A grateful prophet prays a psalm of thanks.	An angry prophet prays prayers of lament.

This suggested structure alone doesn't necessarily mean that the Ninevites definitely came to faith in Yahweh, with the little they had been told.

However, I believe that the structure of the book as a whole, the wording of verse 5 that they "believed," the resulting actions of fasting and putting on sackcloth (vv. 6–8a) and the call to repentance and prayer (v. 8b), all strongly suggest that the people of Nineveh did, actually, come to faith.

In fact, Dr. Leslie Allen suggests that these parallels between the conversion of the sailors in chapter 1 and that of the Ninevites in chapter 3 are designed to help the Jewish readers of Jonah feel more sympathy for the repentant people of Nineveh.

> The narrator's psychological purpose in drawing this and other parallels with ch. 1 is to induce his hearers to transfer their kindly attitude toward the ship's captain and crew to the king and citizens of Nineveh. Had he begun his story with ch. 3, his aim in telling it would have had no hope of fulfilment. Chapter 1 has served the purpose of softening the reaction of the listening circle toward comparatively innocuous foreigners before confronting them with an odious community of hardcore heathens.[160]

5. Jesus Himself Acknowledges Their Repentance

Finally, Jesus Himself seemed to believe that the repentance of the Ninevites was genuine. Matthew and Luke both recorded in their gospels Jesus's reference to "the sign of Jonah," a statement we will explore more in the final chapter of this book. In that context, however, Jesus then said this:

> The men of Nineveh will stand up at the judgment with this generation and condemn it; for they repented at the preaching of Jonah, and now something greater than Jonah is here. (Matthew 12:41)

Jesus's words lead us to assume that He believed that the people of Nineveh came to faith in God. That is certainly the response He was looking for from the people and leaders of Israel, and it seemed as though Jesus believed that was what had happened through the preaching of Jonah.

So perhaps the Ninevites *did* come to faith in the God of Jonah after all.

Perhaps we should give these repentant Nazis a little more credit.

Or perhaps we should give God the credit.[161]

After all, as Jonah so eloquently put it in his psalm of thanks, "Salvation comes from Yahweh" (Jonah 2:9).

Some would say that the change in the population of Nineveh was very short lived. We noted back in the first chapter that about a century after Jonah, the prophet Nahum spoke strong words of condemnation to the people of Nineveh for their sins and predicted their conquest by the Babylonians.[162] It seemed to have only taken a few generations for faith in the God of Israel to have disappeared.

That may well be the case. However, that need not call into question the genuine faith of the generation of Ninevites who heard Jonah preach and repented in response.

So to summarize, what I believe we have in this chapter is a reluctant prophet who preached a partial message about the seemingly inevitable judgment of God.

And for the second time in the book, pagan Gentiles came to faith.

Why? Because our gracious God is the God of the second chance.

And He's the God of the second chance not just for runaway prophets.

He's also the God of the second chance for ancient Nazis who put on sackcloth and called on His name.

Yahweh Surprisingly Sees and Relents

So, Yahweh surprisingly called His prophet a second time.

Jonah surprisingly obeyed Yahweh and went to Nineveh.

And the people of Nineveh, surprisingly, listened to the minimalistic preaching of the reluctant prophet and responded.

The final surprising move in this chapter was how Yahweh reacted.

He relented.

Yahweh chose not to send the destruction that He had threatened.

> And when God saw their actions and how they turned from their evil, He relented about the calamity He had threatened and He did not bring it on them. (Jonah 3:10)

One commentator notes, "No fire and brimstone fell on this latter-day Sodom after all."[163]

On one hand, this shouldn't surprise us because this is exactly what God's Word teaches:

> If at any time I announce that a nation or kingdom is to be uprooted, torn down and destroyed, and if that nation I warned repents of its evil, then I will relent and not inflict on it the disaster I had planned. (Jeremiah 18:7–8)

On the other hand, the original Jewish readers of Jonah's story would have been very surprised that Yahweh did not judge the Assyrians for their extreme brutality and wickedness.

As we'll see in the next chapter, Jonah was certainly surprised.

And hugely disappointed.

But while we may celebrate Yahweh's willingness to relent and not bring the promised calamity on these people who had repented, it raises a couple of important questions about two of God's attributes: His *immutability* and His *justice*.

The *immutability* of God simply means that God does not change.

> I, the LORD [Yahweh], do not change. So you, the descendants of Jacob, are not destroyed. (Malachi 3:6)

This is an immensely important characteristic of God that makes Him worthy of our trust and dependence. If God was fickle or changeable, our trust in Him would never be certain. If God always seemed to change His mind, we wouldn't be able to believe what He said.

That is why the Bible often reminds us that God does not change.

> In the beginning you laid the foundations of the earth,
>   and the heavens are the work of your hands.
> They will perish, but you remain;
>   they will all wear out like a garment.
> Like clothing you will change them
>   and they will be discarded.
> But you remain the same,
>   and your years will never end. (Psalm 102:25–27)

> God is not human, that he should lie,
>   not a human being, that he should change his mind.
> Does he speak and then not act?
>   Does he promise and not fulfil? (Numbers 23:19)

> He who is the Glory of Israel does not lie or change his mind;
> for he is not a human being, that he should change his mind.
> (1 Samuel 15:29)

Those final two quotations from Numbers and 1 Samuel do raise questions, however, when they are considered alongside a verse like Jonah 3:10.

Doesn't that seem to suggest that Yahweh does, in fact, change His mind?

How do we reconcile these passages?

What we need to understand is that while God is unchanging in His being and His character and His word, He is still *responsive* to His creatures, particularly when human beings change their behaviour.

Theologian Wayne Grudem helpfully describes God's immutability this way:

> God is unchanging in His being, perfections, purposes and promises, yet God does act and feel emotions, and he acts and feels differently in response to different situations.[164]

In Jonah 3, Yahweh didn't change who He is.

The people of Nineveh changed.

And when they turned from their wickedness and cried out to God, He responded.

The second attribute of God that is often discussed in relation to Yahweh's relenting in Jonah 3 is His *justice*.

God's *justice* means that He always does what is right and good.[165] Numerous verses of scripture also celebrate this divine characteristic.

> Will not the Judge of all the earth do right? (Genesis 18:25)

> He is the Rock, his works are perfect,
>> and all his ways are just.
> A faithful God who does no wrong,
>> upright and just is he. (Deuteronomy 32:4)

> I, the LORD [Yahweh], speak the truth;
>> I declare what is right. (Isaiah 45:19)

And because God is upright and just, He judges sin and wickedness.

But if that's true, how can God forgive bloodthirsty Assyrians?

How can God forgive terrorists who skin people alive, gouge out their eyes, dismember their bodies, and burn their children?

How can a God of justice forgive Nazis?

But before we get too self-righteous, we need to ask,

How can God forgive people who gossip?

How can God forgive those who are sexually immoral?

How can God forgive the proud and self-sufficient?

How can He forgive people who pursue money and power and pleasure and position instead of His glory and renown?

In other words, how does a God of justice forgive any of us for any of our sins, large or small?

The answer is found in the cross.

The Bible makes it clear that when Jesus died on the cross, it wasn't a cosmic mistake or unforeseen horror, but a pre-planned initiative of the triune God.[166] And Jesus wasn't simply showing the extent of God's love for us, or leaving us a good example, although it certainly was both of those things.[167]

It was also much more than that.

On the cross, Jesus paid for our sins as our substitute by taking on Himself the wrath of God against our sin. The apostle Paul said:

> God made him who had no sin to be sin for us, so that in him we might become the righteousness of God. (2 Corinthians 5:21)

What does this have to do with God's justice, and His forgiveness of Assyrian Nazis?

In a profound passage on the cross of Jesus, Paul wrote,

> This righteousness is given through faith in Jesus Christ to all who believe. There is no difference between Jew and Gentile, for all have sinned and fall short of the glory of God, and all are justified freely by his grace through the redemption that came by Christ Jesus. God presented Christ as a sacrifice of atonement, through the shedding of his blood—to be received by faith. He did this to demonstrate his righteousness, because in his forbearance he had left the sins committed beforehand unpunished—he did it to demonstrate his righteousness at the present time, so as to be just and the one who justifies those who have faith in Jesus. (Romans 3:22–26)

In this stunning collection of verses, Paul explained that all those who put their faith in Jesus—both Jews and Gentiles—are justified or declared to be righteous by God because of Jesus's sacrifice on the cross. But notice the comment in verse 25—the cross demonstrates that God is righteous or just, which is important because, in the past, He had left sins unpunished.

This is what had happened to the Ninevites in Jonah—as well as Jonah himself—and countless others through the centuries.

God had graciously chosen to forgive people for their wrongdoing and sin when they turned to Him.

But that left God open to the charge of being unjust.

Imagine being an Israelite in Jonah's time, and the Assyrian army had killed or maimed or raped or kidnapped a beloved family member of your household. And then you heard the story of Jonah, that Yahweh had forgiven the very people who had done this!

How was that right?

How was that fair?

Where was the justice?

What Paul was saying was that God can be forgiving towards sinful people who had done all kinds of horrible things because He knew that Jesus was going to come and pay for those sins.

Jesus was going to absorb God's wrath.

He was going to pay the penalty in full.

That is why Paul noted in Romans 3:26, that because of the cross, God can be both "just and the one who justifies those who have faith in Jesus." New Testament scholar D. A. Carson notes,

Justification is first and foremost about the vindication of God. God simultaneously preserves his justice while justifying the ungodly. That is the heart of the gospel.[168]

This is why our gracious God can be the God of the second chance for a prophet who had run away.

That is why our gracious God was the God of the second chance for a city of barbaric terrorists.

That is why our gracious God is the God of the second chance in my life.

And that is why our gracious God can be the God of the second chance for you.

Because that is who He is.

I Am Jonah

We have covered a lot of ground in this chapter, and it's time to draw it to a close. So once again, I am going to hold off exploring the key idea of this chapter—that **God is the God of the second chance—** for now.

Instead, like the big idea of the previous chapter, I want to come back to these concepts in the last chapter as we focus on Jesus.

In the meantime, as we finish, I'd like to come back to Jonah and briefly explore three more ways we can be like him.

1. I am Jonah when I accept God's grace, but my attitude hasn't really changed.

There is no doubt that Jonah was extremely grateful for the grace of God in his life.

The entire psalm in Jonah 2 makes that abundantly clear.

But there have been numerous hints in the last couple of chapters that suggest that Jonah's heart attitude had still not completely changed.

We observed the strong comparison he drew in his psalm between "those who keep clinging to their useless idols" (Jonah 2:8) and himself (verse 9), as though he was morally superior.

We commented on the fact that in the entire psalm inside the fish, Jonah never admitted that running from God was wrong.

Now we've seen that while Jonah outwardly obeyed the command of Yahweh and preached in Nineveh, he only seemed to preach a strong message of judgment against the city.

All that raises the question—had Jonah really changed at this point?

A few scholars suggest that he had. For example, one writes,

> When Jonah received his second call to Nineveh, he answered it as a man who had been changed by grace ... Jonah is now ready to serve as an instrument fit for God's design in preaching the gospel ... His obedience was defined by his faithfulness to the command of God's Word.[169]

He also quotes approvingly another author,

> As a sinful man, whose sin had been forgiven, [Jonah] could not fail to accept ... the mission now assigned him in a spirit of reverence and dutifulness—of gratitude, submission, and

obedience ... Chastened and subdued, of a meek and quiet spirit, overwhelmingly convinced that no device of man can prosper against the strong hand of the Most High, he would return with a readiness to render implicit and unquestioning obedience to whatever the Divine oracle should enjoin.[170]

Really?

That's not how I read Jonah chapter 3, particularly in light of the observations about his heart listed above.

And it's extremely difficult to maintain the idea that Jonah was "changed" and is "ready to serve," with a spirit of "submission and obedience" considering where the story is going to go in chapter 4. It's hard to claim that Jonah was ready to "render ... unquestioning obedience" when in the very next chapter he did the exact opposite and angrily questioned God's forgiveness and character.

Rather, I think it will be better for us to acknowledge a much less romantic view of Jonah—he was grateful for God's grace, he was thankful to have been saved from drowning and given another chance, but grace still had a great deal of work to do in transforming his character.

And the same is true for all of us.

That's why theologians generally describe sanctification as a process.[171] Sanctification is our "ongoing transformation into greater Christlikeness," and this is "an ongoing work that continues throughout one's life."[172]

The truth is that none of us have arrived yet.

None of us are perfect.

None of us are completely like Jesus.

Rather, just like Jonah, we are a work in progress. If we have the Spirit of God in us, there is no doubt that He is at work transforming our character.[173]

But that doesn't mean we have it all sorted or have all our ducks in a row.

Rather, just like Jonah, we may have accepted God's grace, and yet His grace and His Spirit still have work to do on our attitudes and character.

2. I am Jonah when I obey God, but my heart isn't really in it.

This second observation flows from the first one.

As we have just noted, some scholars suggest that Jonah is a new man in chapter 3, and as proof of that, they point to his obedience to the renewed call of Yahweh. Remember this line? "His obedience was defined by his faithfulness to the command of God's Word."

However, I'm not as convinced that Jonah's obedience to God's call necessarily means he'd had a change of heart.

The Bible makes it very clear that God's people can *outwardly* obey His commands, and yet *inwardly* be far from God.

For example, in the Old Testament, the prophet Isaiah brought a message of condemnation from God because His people were worshipping according to the Law, but their hearts were not really in it.

> These people come near to me with their mouth
>   and honour me with their lips,
>   but their hearts are far from me. (Isaiah 29:13)

Jesus, too, condemned people in His day for seeming to obey scripture but being far from God. Some of His harshest words were spoken against the religious leaders who outwardly obeyed scripture, but inwardly were guilty of hypocrisy.

> Woe to you, teachers of the law and Pharisees, you hypocrites! You are like whitewashed tombs, which look beautiful on the outside but on the inside are full of the bones of the dead and everything unclean. In the same way, on the outside you appear to people as righteous but on the inside you are full of hypocrisy and wickedness. (Matthew 23:27–28)

My reading of Jonah's story suggests he was guilty of the same thing.

Oh, he obeyed the call of Yahweh that came a second time. He went to Nineveh.

But you get the impression he was there under compulsion.

He was a reluctant preacher.

His heart wasn't really in it.

But how often are we the same?

We might give a proportion of our income to God's work as an act of obedience, but how often is our giving *joyous, sacrificial and from the heart?*[174]

We might attend church services religiously, but are we *passionate* about joining with God's people to worship Him?[175]

We may read God's Word regularly, but is it a chore to be checked off our to-do list, or do our hearts *delight* in His Word?[176]

We may do wonderful spiritual acts like giving to the poor, praying, and fasting. But Jesus said if we do that to be seen by others, if our heart isn't focused on honoring and worshipping God alone, there is no value in what we do.[177]

Don't get me wrong; obedience to God's Word is a good thing.

But what God really wants, from all His wayward children, is obedience that flows from a heart devoted to Him.

3. I am Jonah when I only communicate one aspect of the biblical message.

We saw earlier in the chapter that Jonah's message to Nineveh seems to be one of condemnation and judgment.

There seems to be no hope of forgiveness.

There is no message of grace.

In other words, Jonah brought the *bad news* about the Ninevites' wickedness and evil and the judgement of God that was coming as a result. But he failed to also announce the *good news*, that forgiveness and deliverance was available if they repented.

He failed to tell them that Yahweh is the God of the second chance.

A few preachers are still like that today. They passionately declare God's impending judgment on sinners, seeming to delight in their fire-and-brimstone message.

To preach the bad news of God's judgment without the good news of God's love and the grace and forgiveness available through Jesus, is not biblical preaching.

But neither is talking about the good news of God's grace and love without acknowledging the bad news of our sin and God's future judgment if we don't repent.

I sometimes wonder if today our greatest danger is doing the opposite of what Jonah did.

We talk a great deal about the unfailing love of God.

We celebrate the forgiveness that Jesus offers.

We preach about God's grace.

And we should—that is the gospel, the message of good news that has come through Jesus.[178]

But I sometimes wonder whether we, too, only share half the message.

Jonah only preached the bad news and left out the good.

How often do we only preach the good news and leave out the bad?

When Paul brilliantly articulated the gospel of grace in his *magnum opus*, the letter to the Romans, he didn't immediately jump into a description of the wonder of grace. After his introduction, Paul spent almost three chapters showing the sinfulness of all humanity. Here's how he summarized his teaching towards the end of that section, using different quotations from the Old Testament:

> There is no one righteous, not even one;
>> there is no one who understands;
>> there is no one who seeks God.
> All have turned away,
>> they have together become worthless;
> there is no one who does good,
>> not even one. (Romans 3:10–12)

Paul spent three chapters making sure his readers understood the *bad news* of our sin before unveiling the *good news* of the grace that is found in Jesus Christ.

In my favorite book on the grace of God, *Transforming Grace*, author Jerry Bridges uses the analogy of an engaged couple going into a jewelry store to buy a ring. He describes how a jeweler will often use a black cloth as a background for the variety of rings and jewels to enhance the beauty of each one. He writes,

> Our sinful condition hardly qualifies as a velvet pad, but against the dark background of guilt and moral pollution, God's grace in salvation sparkles like a beautiful, clear, and flawless diamond.[179]

Jonah's problem was he only shared the bad news and didn't get to the good news of God's grace.

Our problem is we often jump to the good news, without helping people understand the bad news of our sin and rebellion against God.

---

1. I am Jonah when I accept God's grace, but my attitude hasn't really changed.

2. I am Jonah when I obey God, but my heart isn't really in it.

3. I am Jonah when I only communicate one aspect of the biblical message.

Father,

I am Jonah.

I am very grateful for Your grace in my life, but often, I haven't allowed that grace to completely transform me. All too often, I can be thankful for what You have done in my life, and yet my attitude doesn't reflect that in all areas of my life. I pray You'll help me allow Your grace to affect every facet of my life and character.

Lord, I confess too that many times I do obey You but more out of necessity or a sense of obligation, rather than an overflowing heart of thankfulness. I'm challenged when I think about how often I may perform certain spiritual practices in my life more out of habit, rather than out of an overflowing passion for You.

And, Father, like Jonah, I'm often guilty of only sharing some of the message. It's hard living in a culture that doesn't even believe in sin or ultimate right and wrong. And yet if people are really going to understand the good news of grace, they need to understand the bad news of sin and judgment as well. Help me find ways of sharing all the truths of Your Word in sensitive and compassionate ways.

Amen.

Discussion Questions

1. This chapter talks about the God of the second chance. When have you experienced a second chance from God in your own life?

2. How do you think Jonah might have felt when "the word of Yahweh" came a second time? Relief? Frustration? Resigned? Delighted? Explain your answer.

3. How do you think Jonah might have been feeling as he came within sight of Nineveh, and prepared to enter its gates?

4. Why do you think Jonah only seemed to preach a message of condemnation in Nineveh?

5. Were you convinced by the arguments in this chapter that the Ninevites came to saving faith in God? Why or why not?

6. Have you ever seen someone trust in Jesus, and it completely surprised you? What happened?

7. Some authors suggest Jonah was a changed man in Jonah 3, while this book argues he really wasn't. What do you think? Why?

8. Think of a time when you had an opportunity to talk about God but struggled to do that? Why was that difficult? What would you do differently if you had that opportunity again?

Chapter 5: A Great Anger (Jonah 4:1–4)

And when God saw their actions and how they turned from their evil,
He relented about the calamity He had threatened
and He did not bring it on them.
But to Jonah this was a great evil, and he burned with anger.

Jonah 3:10–4:1

When I first preached through the book of Jonah at our church, we showed a brilliant YouTube video from the Crossroads Kids Club. They have a collection of online videos called *God's Story* that introduce children to various stories and books in the Bible using colorful animation and age-appropriate humor.

Their video "God's Story: Jonah"[180] is a wonderful introduction to the story of Jonah for kids. It lasts under four minutes and, at the end, there's a thirty-second "quick version," that goes like this:

> God told Jonah to go to Nineveh.
> Jonah ran away on a boat.
> Jonah got thrown off the boat to stop a storm.
> Fish swallowed Jonah.
> Three days later, fish threw up Jonah.
> Jonah told the people of Nineveh to stop being wicked, and they stopped.
> God didn't destroy them.
> And that is a part of God's story.

All in all, that's a pretty good summary of the story of Jonah, isn't it?

Except …

It isn't a summary of the whole book of Jonah. When you look closely at the list, you realize that it's actually a summary of chapters 1 and 3. Chapters 2 and 4 don't get a mention.

Now I don't think this is an issue with a kids' video introducing a story of the Bible and choosing to concentrate on the more exciting moments of the narrative.

I *do* think it's an issue if that's how adults view the book of Jonah. And my hunch is that it is. I haven't tested this statistically, but I think if adult Christians were asked to summarize the book of Jonah, many would come up with something like the list above.

There are at least two problems with that.

One issue is that a summary like the one above ignores half the book. And to concentrate only on the main narrative sections of chapters 1 and 3 means we miss half the book's content. As we have seen in the outline of the book, chapters 2 and 4 record Jonah's reaction to God's saving acts, in either thanks (chapter 2) or lament (chapter 4).

And these chapters are absolutely essential to understanding the overall message of this part of God's Word.

Second, it means we then misunderstand the purpose and theology of the book of Jonah.

This book wasn't written to simply tell the story of two groups of pagan Gentiles who repented and came to know Yahweh despite the best efforts of a rebellious prophet.

Rather, the main focus of the book is this wayward prophet who thought he could say "no" to what God had clearly said, then run away from God, and look down on sinful heathens, while failing to acknowledge and confess his own wrongdoing.

That is why chapter 4 of Jonah is so incredibly important.

The story doesn't end at the completion of chapter 3 with the conversion of the Ninevites.

Chapter 4 is where the story of this wonderful book reaches its crescendo.

> Of all the books of the Bible, Jonah has the most unexpected and overlooked final chapter … There is a final, startling chapter in which the real lessons of the entire narrative are revealed.[181]

While the conversion of the sailors and the repentance of the Ninevites in chapters 1 and 3 are wonderful, the main person in the story who needs to be changed by God's grace is Jonah himself.

And it is in chapter 4 that Yahweh finally brought this home to His prophet.

Jonah's Fierce Anger

As we have already seen, there are a number of surprising twists and turns as the book of Jonah unfolds.

Perhaps the biggest shock, however, comes at the beginning of chapter 4. As the previous chapter finishes, the entire population of the great city of Nineveh, "from the greatest of them down to the least" (Jonah 3:5), had turned from their despicable ways in humble repentance.

And in response, Yahweh relented and turned from His fierce anger (Jonah 3:9–10).

So we are left at the end of chapter 3 basking in the feel-good story of a nation's repentance and God's amazing grace.

> All it would take now to complete the story would be a final verse, Jonah 3:11—"and Jonah returned to his own land rejoicing!"[182]

And then we read the opening line of the final climatic chapter.

> But to Jonah this was a great evil, and he burned with anger (Jonah 4:1).

Wait, *what?*

What's going on?

Jonah had just experienced the greatest response ever received by a preacher in history! His words had triggered the greatest revival ever seen. The reaction to his simple message was something every preacher would die for!

And yet it seemed, in response, he was having a meltdown.

> You would think Jonah would explode with joy, right? He had front-row seats to one of the greatest moves of God in human history. But instead, he goes into the adult equivalent of a temper tantrum.[183]

Before we look at *why* Jonah responded in this way, however, I want us to note *how* his over-the-top reaction is described.

There are some exceedingly clever wordplays in this opening verse in the original text.

For one thing, the text suggests that Jonah thought God's actions of forgiveness were evil!

Yes, you read that right—evil!

That is the literal translation of the Hebrew word *raʿah*, a word that can be variously translated as "bad," "displeasing," "harmful," and at times "evil."[184]

It had already been used in the previous verses in chapter 3 to describe the "evil" of the Ninevites (Jonah 3:8) and then the "calamity" (literally the "evil") that Yahweh had turned from (3:10).

Now the word is repeated in Jonah 4:1 to describe the prophet's conclusion about what Yahweh had done—Jonah believed that Yahweh's gracious actions were "evil" or "wrong."[185]

Again, we're meant to see the deep irony of the story. God was going to bring "evil" on the people of Nineveh for their "evil." But because they repented and turned to Him, He relented, but now Jonah thought that was "evil"![186]

Second, this is then highlighted even more by the addition of our key word *gadol* (great), which modifies the word "evil." We have talked about this important word in the introduction, and it is so key in the book of Jonah that I have used it in the titles of each chapter in this book. It has already been used in the narrative to describe the great city of Nineveh (six times), as well as the great wind (Jonah 1:4), the great storm (Jonah 1:4), the sailors' great fear (Jonah 1:10, 16) and the great fish (1:17).

Now, however, it describes how Jonah viewed Yahweh's actions—not just "evil," but also a "great evil."

Jonah thought God's actions were "exceedingly wrong."

In other words, Jonah not only thought that God's act of forgiveness towards the Ninevites was wicked, he also thought that wickedness was as enormous as the gigantic city, the awe-inspiring storm, and the colossal fish!

Wow!

Finally, there is the last word in the verse, *charah*, which I have translated at the beginning of this chapter with the phrase, "he burned with anger." This is because the term comes from a word that means "burning," and therefore describes a "burning anger" or "becoming inflamed."[187]

Once again, this term was also used towards the end of chapter 3, when the king of Nineveh expressed his hope that the citizens' acts of repentance might turn away God's "fierce anger."

So Jonah was now *burning with anger* that Yahweh had turned from His *burning anger*. "Ironically, just as Yahweh quenched His wrath, Jonah has kindled his."[188]

These wordplays accentuate and highlight the shocking contrast between Jonah and Yahweh as this final chapter begins.

A few chapters ago, I noted Tim Keller's suggestion that Jonah bears a striking resemblance to the two lost sons from Jesus's famous parable in Luke 15. In the first two chapters of the book, Jonah looked like the younger son, deliberately disobeying and running as far as possible.

In the second half of the narrative, however, Jonah now looked like the elder son. He was now (outwardly at least) obeying God's commands.

He was doing what he was supposed to, even if it looked somewhat reluctant. Yet when the Father chose to show amazing grace, he erupted in anger.

> Just like the older brother in Luke 15, Jonah bristles with self-righteous anger at God's graciousness and mercy to sinners.[189]

Jonah thought it was *evil* that Yahweh decided not to do something *evil* to the Ninevites because they had been *evil*.

Jonah was *burning with anger* that Yahweh was no longer *burning with anger*!

Jonah was sitting in judgment of Yahweh, the Judge of all the earth.

And in his view, Yahweh had got things very, very wrong.

Jonah's Bitter Prayer

At this point, Jonah then did something that we have only seen him do once in the narrative so far.

He prayed.

This is at least a positive step forward compared with the Jonah we met in chapter 1. At the beginning of the story, Jonah wasn't interested in praying. He just ran. Now at least Jonah was engaging God in conversation about how he was feeling.

But as we read the content of his prayer—what he actually said to God—we're in for another shock.

> And he prayed to Yahweh saying. "O Yahweh, isn't this what I said when I was still in my homeland? This is why I was so quick to flee to Tarshish." (verse 2a)

Wait, *what?*

Why did Jonah flee?

Suddenly, at the end of the book, we are finally told *the reason* Jonah ran way back in chapter 1.

We were not given a reason at the start for *why* Jonah tried to flee from Yahweh.

He just ran.

And the way the narrative unfolded, particularly when we understand the background of the story and just how bad the Ninevites were, the natural assumption was to assume that Jonah ran because he was *afraid.*

Who would want to go and preach to Nazis?

Who would want to be skinned alive?

What sane person would be keen on having their tongue pulled out or their nose cut off?[190]

Didn't Jonah run because he was *afraid*?

That's the assumption that many readers and scholars have made through the years. One author describes it this way:

> The problem was, however, that Jonah was afraid of what would happen to him ... it was a mission that would likely lead him to hostility, imprisonment or even worse, death ... Jonah was intimidated by the threat of harm or evil. Reports of the brutality that took place in Nineveh would have certainly reached Jonah's ears. To hear of a race of people

who would build pyramids of severed human heads outside the city walls of their enemies was reason enough to make Jonah rigid with fear.[191]

Sounds plausible.

Except that the Bible never actually says that Jonah was afraid.

It never describes him as being "rigid with fear."

Others have suggested slightly different reasons for why Jonah ran. For example, in his excellent book *Leading with a Limp*, Dan Allender suggests that Jonah was trying to flee the call of leadership.[192] Later in the book, Allender adds that "Jonah fled to Tarshish to avoid the humiliation of being a prophet to the hated people of Nineveh."[193]

Sounds possible.

Except that, again, the Bible is silent at the beginning on *why* Jonah ran.

Until we get to Jonah chapter 4.

I love the way the NIV 2011 renders that second line in Jonah 4:2. "That is what *I tried to forestall* by fleeing to Tarshish" (emphasis mine).

So now at the end of the story, we find out that Jonah didn't run because of *paralyzing fear*, *feelings of inadequacy*, or *potential humiliation*.

He ran because he was scared that Yahweh would be forgiving!

He ran because he didn't want God to forgive the Ninevites if they repented.

He ran because he would rather those Nazis went to hell.

That is what he admitted in verse 2. Jonah had tried his best to stop the people of Nineveh from even hearing about God's anger at their great sin, *just in case it caused them to repent*. And yet that was exactly what happened!

Jonah had essentially tried to manipulate God and compromise God's plan by running away.

And he had failed.

And then, if that confession wasn't bad enough, Jonah then quoted Yahweh's own words in scripture back at Him in the second half of verse 2.

> I knew that you are a gracious and compassionate God, slow to anger and overflowing in unfailing love, who relents from bringing calamity (verse 2b).

Jonah had just quoted one of the most important theological statements in the entire Bible. The quotation comes from Exodus 34:6–7, and it is Yahweh's self-description of His character and person. This is His "self-disclosure statement, his press release to the world."[194]

Here is the full passage:

> The LORD [Yahweh], the LORD [Yahweh], the compassionate and gracious God, slow to anger, abounding in love and faithfulness, maintaining love to thousands, and forgiving wickedness, rebellion and sin. Yet he does not leave the guilty unpunished; he punishes the children and their children for the sin of the parents to the third and fourth generation.

This is not the place to fully explore the depths of this incredible announcement of Yahweh's character,[195] but notice the repetition of the divine name at the beginning of verse 6, "Yahweh, Yahweh."

This is like Yahweh saying, "This is it. This is the essence of who I am. This is the core of My identity, My character."

And what is Yahweh like at the core of His being?

> As we have already seen, in the Bible a person's name represents them and their character. And here we see God's character: merciful and compassionate, full of grace and truth. What is God like? He's the God who burns with anger, but He's also the God who is slow to anger. He is the God who does not ignore sin, but He's also the God who forgives sin.[196]

The remarkable thing about this self-revelation of Yahweh is that it took place in the context of one of the worst rebellions the nation of Israel ever committed. Exodus 34 is part of the story of the worship of the golden calf (Exodus 32–34), where Moses's brother, Aaron, led the nation in the idolatrous worship of a golden statue in the shape of a bull while Moses was on Mount Sinai, receiving the Law from Yahweh.

Yet against the backdrop of this heinous sin, Yahweh revealed the essence of His character as the compassionate, gracious, patient, loving God.

> It is difficult to overestimate the importance of [these] verses. They are the longest and most complete description of the Lord's character to be found in the Scriptures, and ... later Scriptures frequently return to them.[197]

It is no wonder that many prophets, psalmists, and leaders later in the Old Testament will quote or allude to this pivotal statement about the character of Yahweh.[198]

> It's quite possibly the most quoted passage *in* the Bible, *by* the Bible. The writers of the Bible circle back to this passage

over and over and *over* again. *Dozens* of times. Moses and David and Jeremiah and Jonah—they quote it and allude to it and pray it and sing it and claim it and complain about it, but above all, they *believe* it. This is ground zero for a theology of God.[199]

And in almost every case, when Exodus 34 is quoted later in the Old Testament, it is in a positive light that invites God's people to confess their sin and return to Yahweh.

Or it is used to celebrate the forgiveness they have already received.

For example, Psalm 103 quotes part of this self-disclosure in Exodus 34 and then breaks into a beautiful song of praise about Yahweh's grace and forgiveness:

> The LORD [Yahweh] is compassionate and gracious,
>   slow to anger, abounding in love.
> He will not always accuse,
>   nor will he harbour his anger for ever;
> he does not treat us as our sins deserve
>   or repay us according to our iniquities.
> For as high as the heavens are above the earth,
>   so great is his love for those who fear him;
> as far as the east is from the west,
>   so far has he removed our transgressions from us.
>   (Psalm 103:8–12)

Throughout the Hebrew scriptures, almost everyone thinks it is a wonderful thing that Yahweh is this compassionate and gracious God.

Virtually everyone who quotes the words of Exodus 34 does so with deep delight and worshipful awe.

The *only person* in scripture that cites these words *disapprovingly* is the prophet Jonah.

The *only time* in scripture that Exodus 34 is quoted *negatively* is in Jonah 4.

For Jonah, the idea that Yahweh would be "gracious and compassionate, slow to anger, overflowing in unfailing love" towards the Ninevites was *abhorrent*!

Jonah was appalled at the graciousness of Yahweh.

And this is the deepest irony of the book.

Remember, this is only the second prayer of Jonah in the entire narrative.

The first prayer is his psalm of thanksgiving inside the fish in chapter 2.[200] There, Jonah was full of gratitude at his deliverance. He celebrated the fact that Yahweh is a gracious and compassionate God. He even ended his psalm with the emphatic declaration, "Salvation comes from Yahweh!" (Jonah 2:9).

Now, in chapter 4, Jonah was full of disgust.

He burned with anger at God's graciousness.

He found Yahweh's compassion abhorrent.

He threw Yahweh's own words from Exodus 34 back into His divine face.

Why the dramatic change? Because Jonah was grateful when Yahweh is gracious *to him*. He just didn't want Yahweh to extend that same grace *to others*.

Especially Ninevites.

In other words, Jonah believed that he was worthy of grace, but the Ninevites were not.[201]

What this shows is that Jonah hadn't properly understood grace.

Grace is never given by God to those who deserve it. Grace, by very definition, is bestowed on the undeserving.

That's what makes grace, grace.

And that's what makes Yahweh, Yahweh.

Jonah's Astonishing Request

As Jonah came to the end of his temper tantrum, he had one final thing to say to complete his meltdown.

> So now, Yahweh, take away my life, for to me death would be better than life. (Jonah 4:3)

Once again, Jonah had a death wish![202] He was so angry and disappointed with God that he just wanted to die.

Many commentators see a link here between Jonah and one of the greatest prophets of the nation of Israel, the prophet Elijah.[203] Elijah ministered a century or so before Jonah during the reign of the evil king Ahab.[204] In one of the great stories of the Bible, he led a challenge against the false prophets of the Canaanite god Baal, when Yahweh rained down fire from heaven (see 1 Kings 18).

In the aftermath of that victory, however, Ahab's evil wife, Queen Jezebel, sent a message saying she would have him killed within twenty-four hours (1 Kings 19:2), and in response, Elijah fled for his life to the southern kingdom of Judah.

Exhausted and afraid, Elijah despaired of life.

> Elijah was afraid and ran for his life. When he came to Beersheba in Judah, he left his servant there, while he himself went a day's journey into the wilderness. He came to a broom bush, sat down under it and prayed that he might die. "I have had enough, LORD [Yahweh]," he said. "Take my life; I am no better than my ancestors." (1 Kings 19:3–4)

It seemed that Jonah, outside the walls of Nineveh, was invoking the words of Elijah.

However, the contrast between the two prophets could not be greater.

Elijah had *obeyed* Yahweh's commands at every turn; Jonah had *disobeyed* and run from Yahweh.

Elijah *fearlessly preached* the Word of God and brought Him glory; Jonah had *reluctantly proclaimed* as little as he could with those to whom Yahweh has sent him.

Elijah, while he won the encounter on Mount Carmel, feared that he had still *ultimately failed* to turn Israel back to Yahweh. Jonah, on the other hand, had encountered *unbelievable success*, but was peeved with God about that very fact.

> Jonah is no Elijah, as the listening circle are well aware: the echo of Elijah's prayer is but another nail in the coffin of Jonah's reputation. What religious monster is this?[205]

Yahweh's Searching Question

Jonah's petulant voice finally fell silent, and in the stillness that followed, one single question remained.

How would Yahweh respond to this latest episode from His sulking prophet?

Would Yahweh flare with anger at this insolence? Would He strike out at Jonah for denigrating His character and plans? Would He finally give up on this rebellious, sinful preacher?

The simple answer to all these questions is no.

Yahweh is the God of compassionate, wonderful grace.

He is the God who was gracious with *gentile sailors* who prayed to other gods.

He is the God who was gracious to *ancient Nazis* who mutilated their victims and celebrated it.

And He is the God who was gracious to *His prophet* who got angry with Him and questioned His plans and misused His scriptures.

And so in the silence that followed Jonah's temper tantrum, Yahweh asked a simple question:

> Then Yahweh answered, "Is it right for you to burn with anger?" (verse 4, repeated in verse 9)

In asking this question, Yahweh was showing Himself to be exactly who the Hebrew scriptures claimed Him to be—the "gracious and compassionate God, slow to anger and overflowing in unfailing love."

And Yahweh's question was a beautifully tender response that was designed to help Jonah think about what he was doing and saying.

There are echoes of the story of Genesis in this moment.

When Adam and Eve had rebelled against Yahweh and eaten the forbidden fruit in Genesis 3, Yahweh's response was an equally tender and probing question. "Where are you?" (Genesis 3:9).

Likewise, when their firstborn son, Cain, was burning with anger and jealousy against his brother Abel, Yahweh asked, "Why are you angry? Why is your face downcast?" (Genesis 4:6).

Interestingly, in Genesis 3, Adam responded to Yahweh's question, which began a dialogue between them about what they had done. Conversely, in Genesis 4, Cain refused to respond to Yahweh and instead gave in to his anger and murdered his brother.

In the book of Jonah, the prophet refused to answer God, and ended up looking more like a murderous Cain than a remorseful Adam.

In fact, Jonah still looked like the same petulant prophet who refused to talk to Yahweh at the very beginning of the story. In Jonah 1, when Yahweh first commanded Jonah to go to Nineveh, Jonah had refused to answer Him and instead ran away.

Now in chapter 4, when Yahweh questioned Jonah, once again Jonah refused to answer Him and walked away to a position overlooking the city of Nineveh (verse 5).

It was almost as though Jonah was running away again—if not in distance, certainly in attitude.

As this scene closes, Jonah looked like a pouting toddler stomping his feet and throwing a tantrum in the supermarket aisle.

And Yahweh looked like a patient and loving father, graciously and patiently dealing with His rebellious child.[206]

I Am Jonah

Once more, let's allow Jonah's story to be a mirror of our own lives and our responses to God.

1. I am Jonah when I get angry at God for not doing what I want.

It is very easy for us to read the stories of the Bible, especially when God's people fail dramatically, and shake our heads at their actions.

I've found myself doing it with Jonah in this part of the story.

But before we self-righteously condemn Jonah for his sulking and anger, I think it will be wise to pause and consider the times in our lives when we have gotten angry at God.

We get angry when God doesn't give us that job or promotion we so desperately want.

We get angry when God doesn't miraculously keep that romantic relationship together.

We get angry when God takes that beloved family member home to be with Him.

We get angry when God lets that diagnosis happen and doesn't heal instantly.

We get angry when God lets the business fail and go into bankruptcy.

We get angry when God doesn't bring our teenager back home when we expect.

We get angry when God allows our spouse to walk out of our home and our marriage.

We get angry when that friend who hurt us seems to prosper and be blessed.

We even get angry when God doesn't just "zap" us and fix our anger problem!

If we're honest, we all get angry with God at different moments in our lives.

I got angry at God numerous times during my wife Rochelle's almost twenty-year battle with fibromyalgia. It is a condition similar to chronic fatigue syndrome that also includes varying levels of pain.

Rochelle's health first crashed six weeks after our wedding day. Initially, we thought it was simply exhaustion from wedding prep, moving cities, and farewelling family. However, when her condition didn't improve over the next weeks and months, and she was forced to give up full-time work, we realized this might be a longer-term issue than we had originally thought.

It wasn't until four years later that we finally even got a diagnosis of what was wrong with her—four years without even a name to put to this condition she was suffering.

In the meantime, we began full-time pastoral ministry, changed cities within New Zealand, and then moved to the United States and fast-tracked my seminary studies. We then shifted back to New Zealand, began a new ministry role, started a family, planted a church, and bought and renovated our first home.

But during all that, Rochelle continued to struggle. Some days were good, and the pain was minimal and the fatigue manageable. We were able to serve together in ministry, and on the good days in the States, she was able to audit classes at seminary.

But other days were incredibly hard. She would lie in bed without even the energy to get up and do anything. There were days when I would simply hold her while she cried with pain and frustration.

And I would cry out to God and plead with Him to heal my wife.

I am convinced that God heard every one of those prayers. But it often didn't feel like it. Sometimes it felt like my prayers just bounced off the ceiling. Sometimes it felt like God was ignoring me. Sometimes I echoed the question that the disciples asked Jesus in the middle of a storm. "Teacher, don't you care?" (Mark 4:38).

Have you ever been in a place where you got angry with God?

Confused by God's actions—or inactions?

Wondered about the wisdom of His plan?

Or if He even had a plan? "Lord, don't you care?"

You see, we are a lot more like Jonah than we will care to admit.

We may not pout and sulk and mope as much as Jonah did. But sometimes we get angry too.

And sometimes we run from Him, even if we've never moved physically from where we are standing.

The answer to those times, by the way, is to learn the biblical practice of lament. In his superb book *Dark Clouds, Deep Mercy*, Mark Vroegop defines lament as "a prayer in pain that leads to trust."[207] He adds,

Without lament we won't know how to process pain ... Without lament we won't know how to help people walking through sorrow. Instead, we'll offer trite solutions, unhelpful comments, or impatient responses.[208]

I discovered lament during our time at seminary, during a tough season with Rochelle's health. One beloved professor opened up the psalms of lament in the Old Testament, that provided us with a model and a template for how to honestly bring our pain and confusion to God.

During that season, I particularly fell in love with Psalm 13. I resonated with the questions that David cried out to God in the opening verses.

> How long, LORD [Yahweh]? Will you forget me for ever?
> > How long will you hide your face from me?
> How long must I wrestle with my thoughts
> > and day after day have sorrow in my heart?
> > How long will my enemy triumph over me? (Psalm 13:1–2)

As Vroegop points out in his book, it is not wrong to bring our hurts and pains, even our complaints, to God. That is exactly what the lament psalms do. That is what David did in Psalm 13.

However, in the lament psalms, complaint is only one step in the process of moving from pain to praise.[209] The problem is when we don't continue through the rest of the process. We stop at complaint and become bitter and angry with God.

That was Jonah's problem.

2. I am Jonah when I try to sit in judgment of God.

This is another aspect of Jonah's anger at Yahweh that we need to explore.

As we noted earlier in the chapter, Jonah wasn't just angry at God.

Jonah ended up sitting in judgment of God.

Jonah had arrived at the point where he had decided that he knew better than Yahweh.

In his great wisdom, Jonah was convinced that the Almighty had made a mistake.

An error of judgment.

A miscalculation.

And Yahweh needed Jonah to help Him get it right.

Remember, that was why Jonah said he originally ran away in chapter 1—to ensure that Yahweh didn't make the mistake of being compassionate to Nazis who skinned their victims alive.

And that was why Jonah felt able in chapter 4 to rebuke Yahweh and quote scripture back at Him.

For in his opinion, Yahweh had gotten it really, really wrong.

He thought Yahweh's actions were incredibly evil.

Talk about arrogant!

But here's the question—have you ever stood in Jonah's sandals and decided God had made a mistake?

A few pages back I listed a number of different scenarios as examples of times when we get angry at God, such as when we didn't get that job, or when a relationship or marriage failed, or when we got a poor health diagnosis. But if you stop and think about those scenarios, frequently we end up doing exactly what Jonah did—we sit in judgment of God.

Part of our anger is the natural disappointment and brokenness that we feel when our dreams have come crashing down and when our hopes have failed to eventuate.

That's normal and totally understandable.

We've all been there.

But another part of our anger is that God hasn't done what we wanted, and deep down, we think we know what's best for our lives.

We end up sitting in judgment of God, just like Jonah did.

Many years after Jonah's ministry, Yahweh raised another prophet by the name of Jeremiah. In a well-known story from Jeremiah's ministry, Yahweh commanded him to go down to the house of the local potter.[210] There, Jeremiah observed the potter working at his wheel, but when something went wrong with the pot that was being made, the potter crushed the clay back together and started again. Then Yahweh's word came to His prophet:

> "Can I not do with you, Israel, as this potter does?" declares the LORD [Yahweh]. "Like clay in the hand of the potter, so are you in my hand, Israel." (Jeremiah 18:6)

In fact, the very next verses in this passage are the ones I quoted in the last chapter about Yahweh's freedom to forgive a nation or people when they repent:

> If at any time I announce that a nation or kingdom is to be uprooted, torn down and destroyed, and if that nation I

warned repents of its evil, then I will relent and not inflict on it the disaster I had planned. (Jeremiah 18:7–8)

This same imagery of God being like a potter who has the freedom to work with the clay as He sees fit was also used by the prophet Isaiah.

> You turn things upside down,
>> as if the potter were thought to be like the clay!
> Shall what is formed say to the one who formed it,
>> "You did not make me"?
> Can the pot say to the potter,
>> "You know nothing"? (Isaiah 29:16)

> Woe to those who quarrel with their Maker,
>> those who are nothing but potsherds
>> among the potsherds on the ground.
> Does the clay say to the potter,
>> "What are you making?"
> Does your work say,
>> "The potter has no hands"? (Isaiah 45:9)

These words were then picked up by the apostle Paul in the New Testament, in Romans 9, where Paul quoted from Isaiah's words. But he introduced his quote with a simple but profound question:

> But who are you, a human being, to talk back to God? (Romans 9:20a).

Take a moment to linger with Paul's question. "Who are you, a human being, to talk back to God?"

When life doesn't turn out how we are hoping or praying, it is perfectly natural for us to feel disappointment and angst and frustration and even anger.

And that's what the lament psalms encourage us to bring honestly and authentically to God in prayer.

However, when we sit in judgment of God and assume or assert that God has gotten it wrong, that's when we look just like Jonah.

Arrogant.

Instead, we need to recognize and remind ourselves that God is the potter, and we are the clay. And while it's natural to have dreams and hopes and ideas, we do not see the master plan that God is enacting, and we do not know everything. As Tim Keller wisely wrote,

> One of the reasons that we trust God too little is because we trust our own wisdom too much. We think we know far better than God how our lives should go and what will make us happy … Therefore, because of our deep mistrust of God's goodness and Word, we do everything we can to get out from under his hand.[211]

Maybe that's why Proverbs tells us that trusting in Yahweh with all our hearts also involves not leaning on our own understanding (Proverbs 3:5). We need to lean into God's wisdom rather than our own.

That brings us back to the Old Testament concept of lament. As Mark Vroegop explains in *Dark Clouds, Deep Mercy*, the lament psalms (like Psalm 13) offer a process to walk through our grief and pain and anger. He describes four key elements: turn, complain, ask, and trust.[212]

What is important about this biblical response of lament is that it takes us on a journey of healing towards trust.

> Lament helps us practice active patience … Lament is how we endure. It is how we trust. It is how we wait … Choosing to trust through lament requires that we rejoice without

knowing how all the dots connect. We decide to let God be his own interpreter, trusting that somehow his gracious plan is being worked out—even if we can't see it.[213]

Jonah still needed to learn how to do this.

3. *I am Jonah when I think I'm better than I really am.*

One final facet of Jonah's behavior in this small passage really intrigues me.

It is the observation by several scholars that Jonah seemed to be deliberately invoking the words of the prophet Elijah in saying that he wanted to die.

As we noted earlier, Elijah ministered about a century before Jonah came on the scene.

But Elijah's reputation and legacy lived on.

He was considered among the greatest of Yahweh's prophets.

This was why later it was foretold that the forerunner of the Messiah would come in the spirit of Elijah.[214]

This was why on the Mount of Transfiguration, when three of His disciples saw a glimpse of His glory, Jesus was joined by Moses and Elijah (representing the Law and the Prophets).[215]

And this was why when Jesus asked his closest followers who the crowds were saying He was, one of the options was Elijah or one of the other prophets.[216]

If you were a prophet in ancient Israel, wouldn't you want to be seen as another Elijah?

The problem was, as we have already noted, Jonah was the polar opposite of Elijah.

He was disobedient, reluctant, petulant, aggrieved.

He was no Elijah.

But it seemed as though he wanted people to see him that way.

This also happened with other people through the Bible.

King Saul was so concerned about his reputation and how he looked in front of the people, that even when the prophet Samuel told him that his kingdom would not endure, he still wanted Samuel to appear with him so that he looked good to the crowds.[217]

When they saw the accolades that a man named Joseph received from people due to an act of generosity, a couple in the early church named Ananias and Sapphira decided to sell a piece of property and pretend they were giving the whole amount to God's work.[218]

And in a stinging rebuke of the hypocrisy of the religious leaders, Jesus accused the Pharisees of this same showmanship:

> Everything they do is done for people to see: they make their phylacteries wide and the tassels on their garments long; they love the place of honour at banquets and the most important seats in the synagogues; they love to be greeted with respect in the market-places and to be called "Rabbi" by others. (Matthew 23:5–7)

The truth is that we all wrestle with this desire at one time or another, don't we?

We want to appear better than we really are.

We want to be looked up to by others.

We long to be admired.

But the call of the Bible to followers of Jesus is to continually battle that desire, that ambition.

"Do nothing out of selfish ambition or vain conceit," the apostle Paul wrote to the church in Philippi.[219]

"Do not think of yourself more highly than you ought," he had written a few years earlier to the Romans. "But rather think of yourself with sober judgment."[220]

Like Jonah, I can often be lulled into thinking I'm much better and much more important than I really am.

We are much more like Jonah than we realise.

---

1. I am Jonah when I get angry at God for not doing what I want.

2. I am Jonah when I try to sit in judgment of God.

3. I am Jonah when I think I'm better than I really am.

Father,

I am Jonah.

I confess that when life doesn't turn out the way I want it to, I have often gotten angry at You. When I am in pain, when I am facing deep uncertainty or fear, I can be just like Jonah. And not only have I gotten angry with You, but there are also countless times when I have presumed that I know better than You. It's a brutal thing to admit how arrogant I can be.

Thank You that You don't give up on me in those times. Thank You that You invite me to bring my pain and my hurt, my questions and my confusion, to You whenever I choose. Thank You for the grace of lament and for the models I find in Psalms and elsewhere of people who wept and grieved before You. Please help me learn to do that more often, more frequently, in times of hardship.

And also help me trust You more deeply when I don't understand Your plans. Help me to never presume that I know better than You. Help me instead to trust that Your wisdom and Your goodness are greater than mine and that You alone are worthy of my trust.

Amen.

Discussion Questions

1. Have you ever had a time when you felt disappointed or let down by God? What happened?

2. Jonah's anger at God is a surprising twist in the story. Do you feel some sympathy for Jonah, or is he completely in the wrong? Explain.

3. What exactly was Jonah angry about?

4. Jonah quoted one of the most important descriptions of God's character in the Bible. How have you experienced God's compassion and grace in your life?

5. Jonah seems to have only a partially correct understanding of God's character. In what ways might we have developed a view of God that isn't completely right?

6. Why do you think Jonah just wanted to die?

7. How does the concept of lament, which was introduced in this chapter, fit with the biblical command to not "talk back to God" (Romans 9:20)?

8. How well have you learned the art of lament in difficult times in your life? How might you grow in this important spiritual discipline?

Chapter 6: A Great Lesson (Jonah 4:5–11)

Then Yahweh said, "You have been so concerned about this plant,
which you didn't toil over or make it grow,
and which appeared one night and died the next.
So shouldn't I have concern for this great city of Nineveh,
in which there is more than 120,000 people
who do not know their right hand from their left,
as well as many animals?"

Jonah 4:10–11

Have you ever known you should do something but just can't be bothered?

You know you should head out into the sunshine for a long run or a brisk walk, but you stay sitting on the couch, playing another game on your phone.

You know you should head home from the office and spend time with the family, but you decide to take a quick look at one more project.

You know you should reach out to that friend you hurt with your thoughtless comment and ask for forgiveness, but you're just hoping it will all be swept under the carpet.

You know you should be more careful with your diet as your weight has been slowly climbing, but you go ahead and order takeaways anyway.

You know you should bring Jesus or church into the conversation at the office on Monday morning when everyone's talking about the weekend, but you'd rather just talk about football instead.

The truth is that often we know exactly what we should do.

We just can't be bothered.

In a sense, that was Jonah's problem in this story—he knew exactly what Yahweh wanted him to do. He knew exactly how he should respond. But selfishness had kicked in—Jonah simply couldn't be bothered.

He'd rather be comfortable than obedient.

But Yahweh wasn't comfortable with that.

And that is why, as I noted in the previous chapter, the story of this beautiful book doesn't end with the repentance of the Ninevites in chapter 3, as wonderful as that is.

For the key person who needed to be transformed by God's grace in the story of Jonah was Jonah himself.

We saw in the previous chapter that in the opening verses of Jonah 4, the prophet was having a complete meltdown. Like an over tired toddler having a tantrum in the supermarket aisle, Jonah got hyper angry at God for being gracious and forgiving to the Ninevites.

And when he was finally finished, Yahweh gently asked a simple question: "Is it right for you to burn with anger?" (Jonah 4:4).

But once again, Jonah didn't answer.

It was almost as though he was done with God.

Jonah was running from God all over again, even though this time he was still in the vicinity of Nineveh.

God's Gracious Provision

As the book comes to a close, in the final few verses, Yahweh taught Jonah the profound lesson that is actually at the heart of this wonderful story.[221]

The final scene begins with the petulant prophet setting up camp outside the city of Nineveh.

> Now Jonah left the city and sat down to the east of it. And he made for himself a shelter and sat down in its shade to see what would happen to the city. (Jonah 4:5)

I find this verse fascinating.

What was Jonah doing?

You would have thought that he couldn't wait to get out of there. He never wanted to go to Nineveh in the first place—surely, as soon as he was done with his preaching mission, he would have been looking for the first train out! Why didn't he cut his losses and run?

And that was especially so knowing that Yahweh had relented from His divine anger, forgiven the Ninevites, and told Jonah about it, hence causing Jonah's meltdown.

If Yahweh had already relented, and judgment was no longer coming, why hang around?

Some scholars suggest that the chronology of events had been changed in the final shape of the story, so that, at this moment, Jonah hadn't yet been told that Yahweh had relented and that the fire-and-brimstone show had been cancelled.[222] And while that's a possibility, the most natural way to read the Hebrew text is that each event in this chapter is sequential.[223]

So Jonah knew that Yahweh had relented, and judgment would not come on Nineveh, and yet he still headed outside the city. He set up camp, built some crude kind of shelter, and waited to see what would happen.

But what exactly was he waiting for?

Was he hoping that God's patience and love would run out before the predicted forty days were up?

Was he hoping that God may yet change his mind again?

Was he hoping that the "repentance" of the Ninevites wasn't genuine, and that they'd be back to their old sinful habits before too long?

Or was he hoping that his continued presence outside the city might embarrass Yahweh and perhaps put Him under pressure to give the Ninevites what Jonah believed they truly deserved?

We're not told why Jonah hung around. Once again, we're given no insight in the text of his motivation or thinking.

We're just left with this image of a brooding, sulking prophet staring out across the arid landscape at the city he hated.

In the musical *Les Misérables*, the main character Jean Valjean was stalked through scene after scene by his nemesis, Inspector Javert.[224] Valjean had been imprisoned for nineteen years for stealing a loaf of bread, and in the eyes of the law-abiding Javert, he was and always would be a hardened and unrepentant criminal.

Meanwhile, Valjean, having been shown incredible grace by a bishop when apprehended for stealing the churchman's silver, turned his life around. Years later, he was a businessman, mayor of his town, and the guardian of a young girl. But Inspector Javert could not believe that a criminal like Valjean could ever change and continued to pursue him relentlessly.

Later in the story, Javert was unveiled as a policeman while working undercover and faced being mercilessly executed. When he was rescued and set free by Valjean, the man he had hated and hunted for so long, Javert could not reconcile the change and ended up killing himself in despair.

The law-abiding Javert could never let go of his belief that Valjean would never change.

Like Javert, Jonah could never believe that the Ninevites might have genuinely repented either.

And yet in this chapter, the contrast between the hatred of Jonah and the graciousness of God could not be clearer.

For right at this moment, when Jonah looked unlovable, Yahweh provided the pouting prophet with a welcome and gracious gift.

> Then Yahweh God provided a plant and made it grow over Jonah to give him shade on his head and deliver him from his discomfort. And Jonah was exceedingly happy about the plant. (Jonah 4:6)

That first line is almost a repeat of Jonah 1:17, where Yahweh "provided" the great fish to save Jonah from drowning. Throughout the story, God is presented as the sovereign Creator, fully in control of everything that He has made. And just as He sovereignly "provided" the fish, now He "provided" a shady plant.

Both the fish and the plant were tools that the sovereign Yahweh would use to deliver Jonah from his own pride and sinfulness.

And Yahweh wasn't finished yet—that word "provide" is going to crop up two more times in the next few verses.

We don't know exactly what kind of plant it was. The Hebrew word used for the plant is only found here in the entire Old Testament. Some scholars suggest it was the castor-oil plant, which grows rapidly in hot climates and has large leaves for shade.[225] Others suggest it was a vine or a gourd.[226]

But ultimately, it isn't important what the plant is, just as the exact species of fish doesn't really matter in chapters 1 and 2. What is key is that Yahweh provided this plant to give shade for Jonah.

(By the way, this suggests that the structure that Jonah had made wasn't doing a great job of keeping the desert sun away. Jonah obviously wasn't much of a handyman!)

But the plant provided Jonah with the additional shade he needed, and it was able to "deliver him from his discomfort."

And notice Jonah's response at the end of verse 6. My translation says that he was "exceedingly happy." The NIV reads that he was "very happy."

It's one of the last appearances of our key word *gadol* (great). This time it was Jonah's delight over the plant that was "great" —he was incredibly happy. His delight was enormous!

In addition, the Hebrew text repeats the word for happiness. Literally it reads, he "was happy with great happiness."[227]

In other words, Jonah was ecstatic!

He was rapt!

He was delighted!

Finally, something had gone right for him!

And the contrast with the beginning of the chapter could not be starker.

Back in verse 1, thinking about the city of Nineveh, Jonah was "burning with anger."

Now, as he enjoyed the comfort and relief of this plant that had spontaneously grown up, he was "happy with great happiness."

Jonah had gone from one extreme to another, from a complete downer to absolute delight.

But this stunning contrast in his emotions says something pathetically sad about his priorities. At the beginning of the chapter, he was red-hot angry at Yahweh's gracious forgiveness of the hated Ninevites. Now just a few verses later, he was totally over the moon about a simple plant that had shot up to give him shade from the desert heat.

Jonah's priorities seemed strangely out of whack.

God's Gracious Destruction

Having made Jonah's day with His gift of a plant, Yahweh now initiated the next part of His object lesson.

> Then God provided a worm at first light the next day, and it attacked the plant so that it withered. Then once the sun had risen, God then provided a scorching east wind, and the sun blazed on Jonah's head so that he felt faint. And Jonah said to

himself, "I just want to die; to me death would be better than life." (Jonah 4:7–8)

The same God who graciously provided a fish (Jonah 1:17) and a plant (Jonah 4:6) now sovereignly provided two further gifts—a hungry worm that chewed the plant and caused it to wither and die (Jonah 4:7), and a scorching east wind that then worked with the desert sun to give Jonah heatstroke (Jonah 4:8).

Why was Yahweh doing this? Why was Yahweh now making Jonah's life miserable?

Was this God simply being vindictive?

Had God simply had enough of this pitiful prophet?

No, this is the same gracious and relentless God we saw in Jonah 1, who lovingly disciplines His children. We have learned back in chapter 2 that God graciously and relentlessly pursues those who are truly His, and a "but Jonah …" is never the final word of the story.

Yahweh was still pursuing His prophet, and this time, a worm and a wind were part of the object lesson.

So poor Jonah sat in his woefully inadequate shelter, as the plant withered and died, the sun mercilessly beat down, and the hot "sirocco" east wind scorched the landscape.

> Along comes the sirocco at [God's] command and blows its hot breath through the loosely woven shelter till it feels like an oven. The blazing sun beats down on Jonah's poor head, now bereft of the friendly *ricinus* plant. Enervated by sunstroke and exasperated by the loss of his plant, Jonah's recent zest for life shrivels like the *ricinus* leaves.[228]

So a day after being "happy with great happiness," Jonah had once again had enough, and at the end of verse 8, he repeated the last part of his death wish from verse 4: "to me death would be better than life."

And once again, Yahweh graciously responded with a simple question. In fact, it was exactly the same question He had already asked Jonah back in verse 4, with three additional words:

> Then God said to Jonah, "Is it right for you to burn with anger over the plant?" (Jonah 4:9a)

This repeated question shows not only the patience and compassion of God toward Jonah but also His wisdom and insight into the idolatry and pride of Jonah's heart. By asking the same probing question twice, with only one subtle difference, Yahweh was about to expose the hypocrisy of Jonah's heart like a skilled surgeon.

Notice the two questions:

> Is it right for you to burn with anger? (Jonah 4:4).
> Is it right for you to burn with anger *over the plant*? (Jonah 4:9; emphasis mine)

The only difference between the questions is that the first time, Yahweh left the focus of Jonah's anger undefined. This second time, He specifically asked about Jonah's anger over the demise of the plant.

But by doing this, Yahweh was highlighting the prophet's double standard.

You see, the first question was about the city of Nineveh and Jonah's anger that Yahweh had decided not to destroy it in righteous wrath. *Jonah was angry about Nineveh because it was* not *destroyed.*

The second question, however, focused on Jonah's beloved plant that he had enjoyed for one day. But the situation was reversed: *Jonah was angry about the plant because it* was *destroyed.*

And what God was doing in asking this repeated question was shining the light of truth on Jonah's double standard. He was trying to show Jonah that his priorities were completely upside down. On one hand, the prophet absolutely hated the people of Nineveh and wanted God to fry them, but on the other hand, he was absolutely devastated when his precious plant died.

He wanted Yahweh to show no mercy to the people of Nineveh, but when He showed no mercy to the plant, Jonah was heartbroken.

And here was the tragedy that Yahweh wanted Jonah to see—Jonah was more concerned about a leafy plant than people who were made in God's image.

But it was not simply a plant. It was what the plant represented.

Jonah was more concerned about his own comfort than the lives of thousands of people.

Did Jonah get it? Did the penny finally drop, as Yahweh repeated His question? Did Jonah finally see the disparity between his feelings about the Ninevites on one hand and a plant on the other?

Sadly, his response to Yahweh's second question showed that he still didn't get it:

> Then God said to Jonah, "Is it right for you to burn with anger over the plant?"
> Jonah answered, "It is right! I am so angry I could die!"
> (Jonah 4:9)

Jonah still looked like the pouting toddler, angry and confused that his every whim was not being catered to. And so as the story drew to a close, Yahweh now explicitly shared the lesson that lay at the heart of the story—the lesson that the runaway prophet had still not grasped.

God's Gracious Lesson

The final words of the book of Jonah belonged to Yahweh.

> Then Yahweh said, "You have been so concerned about this plant, which you didn't toil over nor make it grow, and which appeared one night and died the next. So shouldn't I have concern for this great city of Nineveh, in which there is more than 120,000 people who do not know their right hand from their left, as well as many animals?" (Jonah 4:10–11)

Yahweh now explicitly compared the warped values of Jonah with His own grace and forgiveness.

At the heart of this comparison is the repeated word, "concerned." This word literally means "to have tears in one's eyes," and is often translated as having "pity" or "compassion."[229]

Tim Keller writes, "[It] is a word that means to grieve over someone or something, to have your heart broken, to weep over it."[230] He then goes on,

> For God to apply this word to himself is radical. This is the language of attachment. God weeps over the evil and lostness of Nineveh ... Most of our deepest attachments as human beings are involuntary. We need many things, and we get emotionally attached to things that meet those needs. God, however, needs nothing. He is utterly and perfectly happy in himself, and he doesn't need us. So how could he get attached

to us? The only answer is that an infinite, omnipotent, all-sufficient divine being loves only voluntarily ... It means he voluntarily attaches his heart.[231]

This is the heart that Yahweh exhibited through the Old Testament for His people, Israel. For example, in Ezekiel 20, Yahweh looked back on the way that Israel rebelled during the Exodus and the wilderness wanderings. He said through Ezekiel,

> They rejected my laws and did not follow my decrees and desecrated my Sabbaths. For their hearts were devoted to their idols. Yet I looked on them with pity and did not destroy them or put an end to them in the wilderness. (Ezekiel 20:16–17)[232]

Or He sang about His people on whom He must bring judgment:

> How can I give you up, Ephraim?
>> How can I hand you over, Israel?
> How can I treat you like Admah?
>> How can I make you like Zeboyim?
> My heart is changed within me;
>> all my compassion is aroused. (Hosea 11:8)

This was Yahweh being exactly who He had revealed Himself to be in Exodus 34, as Jonah himself acknowledged—"a gracious and compassionate God, slow to anger and overflowing in unfailing love, who relents from bringing calamity" (Jonah 4:2).

And of course, this image of a God who grieved and who wept over His people was powerfully illustrated by Jesus Himself as he drew near to Jerusalem in the final week before His crucifixion. "As he approached Jerusalem and saw the city, he wept over it" (Luke 19:41).

So what Yahweh was contrasting in these final words of the book of Jonah was the stark difference between what He was compassionate about, as a gracious and loving God, and what moved and concerned His prophet.

There was a world of difference between Yahweh's compassion and Jonah's.

Yahweh highlighted at least four key differences between them.

First, their values were different in terms of their *focus*.

Jonah was concerned about "this plant" (v. 10), although it was clear from the way the story unfolded that it was actually his own comfort and well-being that he was most concerned about.[233]

Yahweh, on the other hand, was compassionate toward "this great city of Nineveh" (v. 11), which really meant all the people in that city who were created in His image. While Jonah was focused on a *thing*—a plant—Yahweh's concern was *people*.

Second, there was a difference in *quantity*.

Jonah was compassionate towards a single plant, while Yahweh had compassion on a city numbering over 120,000 people.

There is some debate over the population of Nineveh here, particularly the phrase, "who do not know their right hand from their left." This phrase often has moral overtones elsewhere in the Bible, where God's people are told to not turn from God's Law to either the right or to the left.[234] In light of that, some have taken the phrase to be a reference to the number of children in the city, who may not have fully known the difference between right and wrong.[235] However, that would mean

Nineveh's population would have been huge, far exceeding what most scholars and archaeologists believe it to have been.[236]

Therefore, most scholars believe that Yahweh was talking about the total population of Nineveh numbering over 120,000 people, and was highlighting the fact that, while the Ninevites were not innocent in terms of their sinful acts, they had no comprehension of God and no way of knowing how to turn to Him without intervention.[237]

Yahweh's point was that the sheer number of people in Nineveh under God's judgment should have evoked in Jonah some kind of compassion or pity.

And if that was beyond him, Yahweh added in the final line of verse 11, "Can't you at least have compassion on the innocent animals of Nineveh? If you can pity one plant, Jonah, can't you pity the numerous cows and dogs and chickens of Nineveh?"

Third, Yahweh also reminded Jonah that there was a significant difference in their *personal investment.*

Jonah had compassion for this single plant, "which you didn't toil over nor make it grow, and which appeared one night and died the next" (verse 10). In other words, Jonah had invested nothing in the plant—he didn't buy it from the local plant nursery, sow it carefully, water it diligently, or watch over it. He had had nothing to do with the growth of the plant—it simply grew up one day and died the next—and yet Jonah was heartbroken over its demise.

The contrast with Yahweh is not spelled out per se in verse 11, but the point is clear—Yahweh was deeply invested in the people of Nineveh. As their Creator, they were part of the world that He made and loved. He had shaped each of them; each Ninevite was made in the divine image and had value and dignity.

Didn't it therefore make sense that Yahweh had compassion on them, His creatures?

Finally, Yahweh was drawing a huge contrast in the *direction* of their compassion.

As we have seen, Jonah's pity for the plant was really a concern for himself and his own comfort. One commentator notes that this shows that Jonah was continuing throughout the story to turn *inward* toward himself and his own needs and desires.[238]

Yahweh, on the other hand, was *outwardly focused*. He was concerned not about Himself but about all those in the book who needed His grace—the pagan sailors, the sinful Ninevites, and even His selfish prophet.

Thus, Yahweh's desire in asking this final question was to open the eyes of His self-centered spokesman to understand His great heart for lost and broken people so that Jonah would join Him in having that kind of heart for pagan people far from God.

Yahweh wanted His prophet to share His heart for lost and sinful people.

I love the way Dr. Jay Sklar paraphrases Yahweh's words in these final verses:

> Nineveh has more than 120,000 people in it! People made in my image! And they are utterly lost, with no idea of what is right and wrong; they are like little children who cannot even tell the difference between their right hand and their left. And even if you do not care about the people, just think about all those animals!
>
> So go ahead, put your plant on one side of a scale and all these things on the other side. Which is weightier? Which matters

more? If you can feel sorry for this meagre and meaningless plant, should I not feel sorry for all these people made in my image? Jonah, do you not get it?! Are not the animals of the city alone worth more pity than your puny plant?[239]

This question from Yahweh is where the story ends, with no recorded response from Jonah.

When I preached this final part of the story, I invited people to look at Jonah's reaction in verse 12. But it's a trick. There is no verse 12. The story simply ends with Yahweh's final question to Jonah, without telling us Jonah's response.

Most writers on Jonah believe this is deliberate.[240]

We have no idea what Jonah said. And so it leaves us pondering how he might have responded.

It's also a deliberate way of inviting us into the story—how would we answer Yahweh?

What will our response be?

How do we respond to the compassion and grace of God in relation to the people around us?

> The story is left unfinished. But, in fact, that is the whole point of its writing ... It carries no conclusion because it summons us to write the final paragraph. It remains unfinished, in order that we may provide our own conclusion to its message. For you are Jonah; I am Jonah.[241]

I Am Jonah

So for the final time, let us ponder the ways in which we can be just like Jonah and accept the invitation at the end of the book to respond to God's grace.

1. I am Jonah when my comfort is more important than God's mission.

We noted earlier in this chapter that Jonah had a huge emotional connection to the plant that grew up and covered his shelter.

When it first sprouted and then flourished, he was "happy with great happiness" (verse 6).

When it subsequently withered and died, he was devastated and wanted to die (verse 9).

But as we noted, Jonah wasn't concerned about the plant per se—it was what the plant provided.

Shelter.

Comfort.

Relief.

Jonah's concern throughout chapter 4 was about *his* plant, *his* shade, *his* personal comfort. There was an inherently selfish streak to Jonah's whole demeanor and attitude.

That's the complete opposite to Yahweh's divine heart for the people of Nineveh as He pointed out in His final words in verses 10–11.

Yahweh is the God who has compassion for sinners who are lost.

What about us? Do we have a heart like Yahweh's for people all around us who are lost in their sin and brokenness? Do we have a longing to see people find Jesus? Do we care about the lost?

Or like Jonah, are we much more concerned about our own comfort, our agenda, our plans, our hopes and dreams than about lost people all around us?

I find this reflection the most personally challenging in the whole book. I am not a natural evangelist; I don't have that spiritual gift. I've never felt skilled at sharing my faith. And like many others, I'm often scared about bringing Jesus into a conversation. And this final climactic lesson convicts me deeply.

In the 2007 song "Hosanna" by Hillsong United from Sydney, Australia, there is a line that says,

> Break my heart for what breaks yours,
> Everything I have for your kingdom's cause.[242]

The sad truth of the story is that right through his story, Jonah acted in the exact opposite way of those lyrics—his heart wasn't broken by what broke God's heart. He wasn't moved by the condition of pagan or sinful people around him.

God's heart is broken by sinners who are far from Him.

God's heart is moved when He eventually must bring judgment and wrath because He is holy.

That's why Jesus looked out across the city of Jerusalem and wept (Luke 19:41).

One of the most stunning examples of this kind of heart is found in the apostle Paul. Originally, Saul of Tarsus (as he was known) was a zealous Pharisee who led the persecution of the earliest followers of Jesus.[243] Then he was confronted by the resurrected Jesus, came to faith, and was called to be an apostle to the Gentiles.[244] But even as he ministered over the ensuing years, traveling through the Roman Empire and establishing churches in Gentile areas, Paul's heart was for his fellow Israelites who continued to reject Jesus.

> I speak the truth in Christ—I am not lying, my conscience confirms it through the Holy Spirit—I have great sorrow and unceasing anguish in my heart. For I could wish that I myself were cursed and cut off from Christ for the sake of my people, those of my own race, the people of Israel (Romans 9:1–4a).

Paul's heart broke for lost people but especially for Israelites who rejected the good news of Jesus, their Messiah. He was far more passionate about their eternal destiny than he was about his own comfort or well-being.

What a contrast to Jonah!

Jonah's heart wasn't broken by sinful people. Instead, he was angry when God spared people whom he hated and didn't think were valuable.

Jonah had more compassion and love for a single plant that could enrich his life and make it better than for thousands of Nazis whom he despised.

Now you may be quietly objecting to this point of application. "I don't hate people! I don't want people I know to go to hell! I don't get angry at God when He forgives someone, even if I don't particularly like them."

And perhaps we are not quite as bad as Jonah at this point. Maybe we don't hate or despise people.

But our indifference or lack of concern for lost people can be just as damaging.

Whenever our own comfort is more important than God's mission to a lost world, we are Jonah.

And that leads to our second reflection.

2. I am Jonah when I love things more than people.

This point follows on from the first.

One of the things that Christians in the Western world especially need to recognize is that our comfort is so often driven by the consumerism and materialism that is all around us. Dr. Craig Blomberg has written,

> It is arguable that materialism is the single biggest competitor with authentic Christianity for the hearts and souls of millions in our world today, including many in the visible church.[245]

What that means is that we cannot think deeply about how we might prioritize our comfort over God's mission without also considering our corresponding struggle with materialism.

When I first preached Jonah 4 in my church, I had a large plant standing on the stage. And I went over to the plant and sat down, pretending to be Jonah looking over Nineveh, waiting to see what Yahweh would do. And I talked about how that plant made Jonah's life more comfortable.

And then I pulled out a nice picnic rug to keep the sand out.

And I unfolded a comfortable deck chair to sit on.

And I added a chilled can of soda for some refreshment.

And some sunglasses to protect my eyes from the glaring sun.

Obviously, none of those things were what Jonah had in the story. He didn't run down to the local hardware store or camping shop on his way out of Nineveh to get a few supplies.

But I made the point that when we're talking about loving our comfort more than God's mission and heart for the lost, we have to talk about all our *stuff*. Our comfort, especially in the Western world, is so often tied into our *assets*, our *toys*, our *money*, our *things*.

The larger house.

The new lounge suite.

The bigger smart tv.

The new set of wheels.

The latest gadget from Apple.

(My lovely wife, Rochelle, when she read an early draft of this manuscript, wrote at this point, "What about Samsung?" since she has an Apple phone, and I have a Samsung. I think it's pretty obvious, though, that Apple users have a lot more to repent of than Samsung users!)

That's not to say that any of these things are wrong in and of themselves. The apostle Paul made it very clear in his teaching on wealth that God "richly provides us with everything for our enjoyment" (1 Timothy 6:17). Upgrading the car that's clocking up the miles, purchasing a new phone, or buying a new bed when the previous one is getting old and lumpy is completely fine.

But Paul also made it clear that we can never put our trust or our hope in wealth:

> Command those who are rich in this present world not to be arrogant nor to put their hope in wealth, which is so uncertain, but to put their hope in God, who richly provides us with everything for our enjoyment. Command them to do good, to be rich in good deeds, and to be generous and willing to share. In this way they will lay up treasure for themselves as a firm foundation for the coming age, so that they may take hold of the life that is truly life. (1 Timothy 6:17–19)

Paul here was echoing much of Jesus's teaching on wealth and riches.

> Do not store up for yourselves treasures on earth, where moths and vermin destroy, and where thieves break in and steal. But store up for yourselves treasures in heaven, where moths and vermin do not destroy, and where thieves do not break in and steal. For where your treasure is, there your heart will be also. (Matthew 6:19–21)

> No one can serve two masters. Either you will hate the one and love the other, or you will be devoted to the one and despise the other. You cannot serve both God and Money. (Matthew 6:24)

> Watch out! Be on your guard against all kinds of greed; life does not consist in an abundance of possessions. (Luke 12:14)

> And do not set your heart on what you will eat or drink; do not worry about it. For the pagan world runs after all such things, and your Father knows that you need them. But seek his kingdom, and these things will be given to you as well. Do not be afraid, little flock, for your Father has been pleased to give you the kingdom. Sell your possessions and give to the poor. Provide purses for yourselves that will not wear out, a treasure in heaven that will never fail, where no thief comes

near and no moth destroys. For where your treasure is, there your heart will be also. (Luke 12:29–34)

According to both Jesus and Paul, the answer to the dangers of wealth and possessions is to hold our possessions and money loosely, to give to others generously, and in so doing to invest in the coming kingdom.

Jesus made the point in both Matthew's and Luke's gospels that "where your treasure is, there your heart will be also" (Matthew 6:21; Luke 12:34).

In other words, our heart always shadows our treasure.

Whatever we put our money into, our heart naturally follows. When we buy shares of a certain company, we take a far greater interest in their success than before. When we buy a season membership for our favourite sports team, we are more invested than ever in the results.

In light of that, author Randy Alcorn suggests,

> As surely as the compass needle follows north, your heart will follow your treasure. Money leads; hearts follow. I've heard people say, "I want more of a heart for missions." I always respond, "Jesus tells you exactly how to get it. Put your money into missions—and into your church and the poor—and your heart will follow." Do you wish you cared more about eternal things? Then reallocate some of your money, maybe *most* of your money, from temporal things to eternal things. Watch what happens.[246]

This is a key issue for us to consider as we think about Jonah's compassion and pity for a plant rather than for the people whom God cared about.

Here's the key question: do our bank accounts, spending habits, regular and spontaneous acts of generosity, and investments of time and energy show that we love people made in God's image? Or do they show that we're more concerned with our own stuff, our own lifestyles, our own comfort and pleasure?

UK pastor Phil Moore powerfully phrases a similar question:

> Will we be distracted by the equivalent of Jonah's leafy plant—self-indulgent trinkets that ultimately do not matter—or will we follow the example of Jesus by pouring out our lives for the world?[247]

3. I am Jonah when I forget how deeply God loves sinners.

At the heart of the contrast between Yahweh and His prophet at the end of the book of Jonah is a comparison between their attitudes toward the people of Nineveh.

Jonah hated them. He hated their barbarity. He hated their destructive and torturous practices. He hated how they had treated his people in the nation of Israel.

He wanted them to burn in hell!

On the other hand, Yahweh loved the people of Nineveh. He didn't condone their practices—what they did was undoubtedly evil. But Yahweh loved them; He felt compassion and pity for them.

And that was why He planned to send them one of His prophets—a man named Jonah—to warn them about the consequences of their sin and call them to repentance.

One of the dangers of reading a story like Jonah's is that we can often place ourselves on the wrong side of the narrative.

We read Jonah 4, and we shake our heads in disbelief at Jonah's hatred.

We sigh in disappointment at his self-centered behavior.

We instinctively put ourselves in the story more on Yahweh's side than Jonah's.

And we forget that more often than not, our beliefs and behavior tend to mirror Jonah's more than God's.

We want to think we have a heart like God's for lost people.

We want to think that we are always loving and compassionate and understanding and forgiving, even when people treat us poorly.

But then we get irate when someone makes a joke at our expense.

We get mad at colleagues who steal the credit for our work or who don't pull their weight.

We get frustrated at drivers who pull out in front of us.

We get angry at people within the church who may have hurt us.

We get annoyed by that activist on television who mocks our faith and promotes a lifestyle that is the opposite of what we believe in.

We refuse to talk to that family member who once made a cutting remark.

We leave the church because others there don't implement our suggestions or cater enough for our needs.

We stop catching up with that friend because their habits annoy us.

And in the process, we forget just how much God loves each of those people—enough to step into their world in the person of Jesus, to live and die for them, just as He did for us.

How often do we stop and think about those people—each one of them—as fellow human beings made in God's image and deeply loved by Him, despite their flaws and sins and failings and brokenness? And despite the ways they may have hurt us?

The truth is I am much more like Jonah a lot of the time. And so are you.

4. *I am Jonah when I am grateful for God's forgiveness but unwilling to forgive others or to help them find forgiveness.*

As we come to the end of Jonah's story, we are meant to see this huge irony.

Jonah was a sinner, a rebel, who ran from God.

He was hurled into the sea like a piece of baggage and descended beneath the waves, only to cry out to the very God he had refused to obey, acknowledge, or even pray to.

And amazingly, God heard his prayer and answered it. Yahweh provided the great fish to save Jonah at the last minute, which Jonah then acknowledged with a scripture-filled, heart felt psalm of thanksgiving and praise. The psalm climaxed with the emphatic biblical statement, "Salvation comes from Yahweh!" (Jonah 2:9).

Jonah was a recipient of the incredible, undeserved grace of God and should have been humming the bars of "Amazing Grace" till the end of his life.

However, while Jonah was grateful for God's grace in his own life, he wasn't happy when God showed that same grace to people he felt were undeserving.

That thoroughly ticked him off!

As we saw in the previous chapter, essentially, Jonah believed that he was worthy of Yahweh's grace, but the Ninevites were not.

This meant he completely failed to understand the enormity of God's grace.

And he also failed to grasp the enormity of his need.

His attitude reminds me of a parable that Jesus told about not being willing to forgive someone else. It goes like this:

> Then Peter came to Jesus and asked, "Lord, how many times shall I forgive my brother or sister who sins against me? Up to seven times?"
>
> Jesus answered, "I tell you, not seven times, but seventy-seven times.
>
> Therefore, the kingdom of heaven is like a king who wanted to settle accounts with his servants. As he began the settlement, a man who owed him ten thousand bags of gold was brought to him. Since he was not able to pay, the master ordered that he and his wife and his children and all that he had be sold to repay the debt.
>
> At this the servant fell on his knees before him. 'Be patient with me,' he begged, 'and I will pay back everything.' The servant's master took pity on him, cancelled the debt and let him go.
>
> But when that servant went out, he found one of his fellow servants who owed him a hundred silver coins. He grabbed him and began to choke him. 'Pay back what you owe me!' he demanded.

His fellow servant fell to his knees and begged him, 'Be patient with me, and I will pay it back.'

But he refused. Instead, he went off and had the man thrown into prison until he could pay the debt. When the other servants saw what had happened, they were outraged and went and told their master everything that had happened.

Then the master called the servant in. 'You wicked servant,' he said, 'I cancelled all that debt of yours because you begged me to. Shouldn't you have had mercy on your fellow servant just as I had on you?'

In anger his master handed him over to the jailers to be tortured, until he should pay back all he owed.

This is how my heavenly Father will treat each of you unless you forgive your brother or sister from your heart." (Matthew 18:21–35)

In Jesus's hard-hitting story, the first servant owes an enormous debt of ten thousand talents (which the NIV quantifies as ten thousand bags of gold in verse 24). Jesus's point was that the debt was so gigantic that it could never be repaid in multiple lifetimes, let alone just one.

New Testament scholar Grant Osborne explains that the *talent* was the highest monetary standard at the time, equivalent to six thousand *denarii* (which we're about to look at). He then calculates the cost of the debt in today's world, based on the value of gold, to be a debt of around twelve billion dollars.[248]

Thus, the first servant owes a mind-blowing, earth-shattering, impossible-to-ever-pay-back amount of money.

And the king in the story forgives the debt.

Completely.

The whole lot.

In full.

Interestingly, the king's decision to forgive the debt is based on his pity or compassion for the servant (verse 27), one of the key focal points of Jonah 4.

Then Jesus explained that the first servant was owed a debt by another servant that amounted to a hundred *denarii* (translated as a hundred silver coins in the NIV in verse 28). A *denarius* was a currency equivalent to a day's work by the average laborer.[249] Therefore, this debt of a hundred *denarii* was significant—more than three months' wages. However, it still paled in comparison with the first eye-watering debt, which Osborne estimates to be six hundred thousand times as large![250]

And yet the first servant, who had his colossal debt wiped out in an outrageous act of grace, was not willing to forgive the debt owed to him by the second servant.

The recipient of amazing grace was unwilling to pass on that same grace to someone else.

In Jesus's parable, the key application being made was about forgiving one another. Those of us who have been forgiven our enormous debts of sin by a gracious God should be more than willing to forgive people who may occasionally sin against us.

But I think we can also apply it to the story of Jonah in this way: if God chooses to save us and forgive our foolishness, wickedness, and sin, we never, then, have a right to question who else God may choose to forgive. It's not as though we have the option of weighing our respective "debts" and then sitting in judgment on people whom we consider to be less worthy of God's forgiveness.

Rather, those of us who experienced the salvation of Yahweh and His amazing grace, should be doing all that we can to tell others about this incredibly gracious God.

> As we respond to the loving mercy and amazing grace of God, outreach happens naturally. When we are loved by God and are passionately in love with the Savior, we desire that others come to know the grace we have experienced.[251]

---

1. I am Jonah when my comfort is more important than God's mission.

2. I am Jonah when I love things more than people.

3. I am Jonah when I forget how deeply God loves sinners.

4. I am Jonah when I am grateful for God's forgiveness but unwilling to forgive others or to help them find forgiveness.

Father,

I am Jonah.

As I come to the end of his story, I am humbled at how often I can be exactly like this old prophet. Like him, we are called to be part of Your mission, to share the good news of Jesus with those around us. There are so many in our world today who need to hear of Your grace.

And yet, Lord, so often, I can be just like Jonah, much more concerned with my comfort, my life, my plans, my stuff. It is so easy to get side tracked from what really matter in light of eternity, which are people who are made in Your image. And yet I can be so busy pursuing my next project, looking to make my next purchase, planning my next experience, and putting all my energy to my own agenda.

I confess that I do not always have Your heart for lost people. I don't see the people around me—in my community, at my work, in my family—the way You see them. Lord, break my heart for what breaks Yours. Help me see people with Your eyes and then reach out to them with Your heart, I pray.

Amen.

Discussion Questions

1. Can you think of a time when you just couldn't be bothered doing something you knew to be the right thing? What happened?

2. Why do you think Jonah camped outside the city of Nineveh to see what would happen, instead of just leaving town?

3. Just as He had provided a great fish, Yahweh now provided a plant, a worm, and a wind. How does the book of Jonah remind us about God's sovereignty and power?

4. Jonah 4 shows the prophet's extreme emotional changes, from rage to delight to misery. Why do you think Jonah got so emotional?

5. Does God's decision to destroy the plant and send the east wind suggest that He was being vindictive or mean to Jonah? Why or why not?

6. In the final verses, God challenged Jonah's distress over the demise of the plant. What kinds of petty things can serve like the plant in our lives?

7. How might our lives look different practically if we had the same kind of compassion and love for lost people that God has?

8. As the story abruptly ends, do you think Jonah had learned the lessons that Yahweh was teaching? Why or why not?

Chapter 7: A Greater Jonah

^{41}The men of Nineveh will stand up at the judgment
with this generation and condemn it;
for they repented at the preaching of Jonah,
and now something greater than Jonah is here.'

Matthew 12:41

Outside of the book of Jonah itself and the historical note in 2 Kings 14:25 which we have discussed in the first chapter, the only other references in the Bible to the prophet Jonah come from the mouth of Jesus in the gospels.

On two separate occasions, Jesus referenced Jonah in the context of conversations with the religious leaders who rejected His ministry. The longer conversation is recorded in Matthew 12:38–41 and is repeated (with a few small variations) in Luke 11:29–32. The second occasion comes later in Matthew 16:1–4, where a similar confrontation took place, and a key phrase about "the sign of Jonah" was repeated by Jesus.

For our purposes in this final chapter, the first incident recorded in Matthew 12 is the most significant. It reads like this:

> Then some of the Pharisees and teachers of the law said to him, "Teacher, we want to see a sign from you."

> He answered, "A wicked and adulterous generation asks for a sign! But none will be given it except the sign of the prophet Jonah. For as Jonah was three days and three nights in the belly of a huge fish, so the Son of Man will be three days and three nights in the heart of the earth. The men of Nineveh will stand up at the judgment with this generation and condemn it; for they repented at the preaching of Jonah, and now something greater than Jonah is here. The Queen of the South will rise at the judgment with this generation and condemn it; for she came from the ends of the earth to listen to Solomon's wisdom, and now something greater than Solomon is here." (Matthew 12:38–42)

In both Matthew 12 and 16, Jesus's words were in response to the religious leaders who asked for a miraculous sign to prove His claims and identity. While this may look innocent or even virtuous, in reality, it was simply part of an ongoing campaign of opposition and rejection by the religious leaders throughout Matthew 12.

By now in His ministry, Jesus had already performed an abundance of miracles that authenticated His claims. When the Pharisee and teacher Nicodemus came at night to talk with Jesus early in John's gospel, he acknowledged that from the outset:

> He came to Jesus at night and said, "Rabbi, we know that you are a teacher who has come from God. For no one could perform the signs you are doing if God were not with him." (John 3:2)

The request of the religious leaders—Jesus' opponents—for yet another miraculous sign was therefore not a positive acceptance of potential faith but an indication that they were looking for more evidence to condemn Him.

This final controversy passage of chapters 11–12 shows further the absolute rejection of Jesus by the leaders. Their demand for a sign demonstrates their rejection of all the previous miracles and ministry of Jesus. His deeds and words were more than enough to prove to anyone who was open that he was the Messiah sent from God.[252]

In response, Jesus called them "a wicked and adulterous generation" (verse 39). This wasn't simply a phrase that popped into Jesus's mind in a moment of frustration or anger. It was deliberately taken from the earliest section of the Old Testament, as the Jewish religious leaders would have fully understood.

In the ancient book of Deuteronomy, as Moses looked back on the rebellion of the previous generation of Israelites in the wilderness, he reminded their children,

> When the LORD [Yahweh] heard what you said, he was angry and solemnly swore: "No one from *this evil generation* shall see the good land I swore to give your ancestors, except Caleb son of Jephunneh. He will see it, and I will give him and his descendants the land he set his feet on, because he followed Yahweh wholeheartedly." (Deuteronomy 1:34–36; emphasis added)

Then toward the close of his farewell sermon, Moses used a similar phrase:

> They are corrupt and not his children;
>   to their shame they are *a warped and crooked generation.*
> Is this the way you repay the LORD [Yahweh],
>   you foolish and unwise people?
> Is he not your Father, your Creator,

who made you and formed you? (Deuteronomy 32:5–6;
emphasis added)

In calling His opponents "a wicked and adulterous generation," then,
Jesus was comparing them to the faithless Israelites who failed to trust
Yahweh and enter the land of promise.

It was at this moment that Jesus invoked the story of Jonah, suggesting
that Jonah was, in some sense, a sign pointing toward Jesus Himself
and proclaiming that the people of Nineveh would stand up at the last
judgment before God to condemn the Israelite leaders of Jesus's day.

Why? Because "something greater than Jonah is here" (verse 41).

In other words, if the people of Nineveh were willing to repent at the
preaching of a wayward, disobedient prophet, how much more should
those who were listening to Jesus be willing to repent at His words?

It's a simple argument from the least to the greatest:

Jesus > Jonah

So as we conclude the story of Jonah, I want to consider how Jonah
points us toward Jesus and why Jesus is greater than Jonah in every way.

Let me suggest four areas in which **Jesus > Jonah**.

Jesus is Greater in His Obedience

It almost feels like an understatement to point out that Jonah was a
disobedient prophet.

From him initially running from God to refusing to pray on the
ship, from arrogantly comparing himself with pagans in his psalm to

reluctantly preaching a truncated message of judgment in Nineveh, from getting hyper angry at God for His graciousness to the Ninevites to selfishly getting upset over a single plant, it's difficult to think of any moment in the entire book when Jonah comes across as a godly, successful, obedient prophet.

There are no moments when Jonah's character reflects graciousness or beauty.

One writer points out that Jonah really is in a category all his own.[253] In scripture, prophets were either considered to be true prophets of Yahweh or false prophets. These were the two possible categories: were they true prophets whose words came to pass, or were they false prophets whose words proved to be untrue?[254]

Jonah was undoubtedly a true prophet. That's certainly how he is presented in 2 Kings 14:25—as Yahweh's "servant," a common designation for His prophets.

And yet Jonah was disobedient and sulky and angry and discontented.

> Thus, the reader encounters in the book of Jonah not merely a true prophet or a false prophet but a *disobedient true prophet*. This was totally unprecedented ... The idea of a *disobedient true prophet* is completely unexpected and creates a sense of suspense and adventure for the reader. Much like a Steve McQueen or Clint Eastwood character in the movies, it is difficult to tell whether Jonah is a good guy or a bad guy.[255]

Jesus could not be more different from Jonah in terms of His obedience to the Father.

For example, this is one of the key themes of John's gospel. Time and again in the fourth gospel, Jesus affirmed that He had come to do the Father's will and that He was completely obedient.

> Very truly I tell you, the Son can do nothing by himself; he can do only what he sees his Father doing, because whatever the Father does the Son also does. (John 5:19)

> All those the Father gives me will come to me, and whoever comes to me I will never drive away. For I have come down from heaven not to do my will but to do the will of him who sent me. (John 6:37–38)

> So Jesus said, "When you have lifted up the Son of Man, then you will know that I am he and that I do nothing on my own but speak just what the Father has taught me. The one who sent me is with me; he has not left me alone, for I always do what pleases him." (John 8:28–29)

> For I did not speak on my own, but the Father who sent me commanded me to say all that I have spoken. I know that his command leads to eternal life. So whatever I say is just what the Father has told me to say. (John 12:49–50)

This continual obedience to the Father was exemplified in the Garden of Gethsemane the night before Jesus died. Facing the impending agony and anguish of the cross in the coming hours, Jesus cried out to the Father for this cup of suffering to be removed.

> He took Peter and the two sons of Zebedee along with him, and he began to be sorrowful and troubled. Then he said to them, "My soul is overwhelmed with sorrow to the point of death. Stay here and keep watch with me."

> Going a little farther, he fell with his face to the ground and prayed, "My Father, if it is possible, may this cup be taken from me. Yet not as I will, but as you will." (Matthew 26:37–39)

It wasn't just the physical pain and torment of crucifixion that Jesus knew was coming.

It was also drinking the cup.

Many of the Old Testament prophets and writers used a metaphor of a cup to describe the wrath and anger of God at the sin and disobedience of His people.

> In the hand of the LORD [Yahweh] is a cup
>   full of foaming wine mixed with spices;
> he pours it out, and all the wicked of the earth
>   drink it down to its very dregs. (Psalm 75:8)

> This is what the LORD [Yahweh], the God of Israel, said to me: "Take from my hand this cup filled with the wine of my wrath and make all the nations to whom I send you drink it. When they drink it, they will stagger and go mad because of the sword I will send among them." (Jeremiah 25:15–16)

This was the cup that Jesus knew He would drink in the coming hours—the cup of God's wrath against sin. All of humanity's sin and wretchedness, collected into a single vile cup.

It was no wonder Jesus asked for there to be another way.

And yet He was still willing to obey.

Even in this darkest of hours, while asking if this cup of suffering could be taken away, Jesus still committed Himself to doing His Father's will.

No matter the cost, Jesus was fully obedient to the Father.

Utterly unlike Jonah.

Jesus > Jonah.

Jesus is Greater in His Compassion

Jonah was not only a wildly disobedient and discontented prophet.

He was also a hateful one.

Jonah hated his enemies.

As we have seen, Jonah scathingly threw the Bible's most-quoted description of God's character right back in His face. "I knew that you are a gracious and compassionate God, slow to anger and abounding in love, a God who relents from sending calamity" (Jonah 4:2).

The tragedy is that the portrait of Jonah is the complete opposite of Yahweh's—an ungracious and hate-filled prophet, quick to blow up with anger, deeply inhibited in his capacity to love, and one who delighted in the severest judgment being poured out on his enemies and those he despised.

Again, there couldn't be a greater difference between Jonah and Jesus.

When the New Testament gospels describe the ministry of Jesus, it is no coincidence that they highlight Jesus's *compassion* toward the broken. For example, in Matthew's gospel alone, we read,

> When he saw the crowds, *he had compassion on them,* because they were harassed and helpless, like sheep without a shepherd. (Matthew 9:36; emphasis added)

> When Jesus landed and saw a large crowd, *he had compassion on them* and healed those who were ill. (Matthew 14:14; emphasis added)

> Jesus called his disciples to him and said, *"I have compassion for these people;* they have already been with me three days

and have nothing to eat. I do not want to send them away hungry, or they may collapse on the way." (Matthew 15:32; emphasis added)

Jesus had compassion on them and touched their eyes. Immediately they received their sight and followed him. (Matthew 20:34; emphasis added)

It's no wonder that Matthew would quote one of the famous prophecies of Isaiah about the coming Servant of Yahweh and apply it to Jesus (Matthew 12:17–21):

> Here is my servant, whom I uphold,
>   my chosen one in whom I delight;
> I will put my Spirit on him,
>   and he will bring justice to the nations.
> He will not shout or cry out,
>   or raise his voice in the streets.
> *A bruised reed he will not break,*
>   *and a smoldering wick he will not snuff out.*
> In faithfulness he will bring forth justice;
>   he will not falter or be discouraged
> till he establishes justice on earth.
>   In his teaching the islands will put their hope
>   (Isaiah 42:1–4; emphasis added).

Unlike His wayward prophet, Jesus was moved with compassion for broken and hurting people.

And this was why the crowds flocked to Him. As they watched Jesus heal and listened to Jesus teach, they saw and experienced the love and grace of God.

They saw and experienced **the God of the second chance**.

They listened as Jesus taught this radical call to love even those who hate you and persecute you.

> If you love those who love you, what credit is that to you? Even sinners love those who love them. And if you do good to those who are good to you, what credit is that to you? Even sinners do that. And if you lend to those from whom you expect repayment, what credit is that to you? Even sinners lend to sinners, expecting to be repaid in full. But love your enemies, do good to them, and lend to them without expecting to get anything back. Then your reward will be great, and you will be children of the Most High, because he is kind to the ungrateful and wicked. Be merciful, just as your Father is merciful. (Luke 6:32–36)

But they not only heard Jesus teach this radical ideology—they also saw Him live it out.

Jesus sought out notorious sinners and invited them to follow Him as disciples.[256]

He hung out at dinner parties with people whom other religious leaders looked down on.[257]

Jesus spoke with outcasts whom a Jewish rabbi would never ordinarily converse with.[258]

Jesus declared that people's sins were graciously forgiven.[259]

Jesus reached outside His own ethnic group of Israelites to people of other ethnicities.[260]

Jesus comforted a repentant thief beside Him on the cross and gave him an undeserved ticket to paradise.[261]

And when He commissioned His disciples after the resurrection, He specifically said that His message of salvation was to go out to all nations, to the ends of the earth.[262]

Many of these examples were people whom the religious leaders of Jesus's day looked down on. Like Jonah, they didn't consider these "sinners" to be worthy of God's love and grace.

But as we've seen throughout the story of Jonah, **we can never run so far, we can never fall so deeply, we can never fail so often, that we are beyond crying out to God**.

And that was what people saw in Jesus—not just a greater obedience to His Father but also a greater compassion and love for people.

Jesus > Jonah.

But it's not simply that Jesus was a more compassionate teacher and prophet.

Rather, it's that, as Jesus stepped onto the stage of human history, we saw the compassionate and gracious God of Exodus 34 in human flesh.

Jesus Is Greater in His Preaching

We noted in chapter 4 that even when Jonah obeyed God the second time and went to Nineveh, it seemed as though he preached reluctantly.

And whether the brief message recorded in Jonah 3:4 is simply a summary of a longer sermon, or the sum total of what he shared, it seemed he simply preached a message of condemnation and judgment.

There was no description about the God who had sent him.

There was no explanation about why judgment was coming.

And there was no comment about how the people could escape this impending doom.

Jonah simply refused to preach grace.

Once again, the difference between Jonah and Jesus could not be starker.

That's not to say that Jesus didn't preach about sin and judgment or warn people of God's wrath.

In Jesus's famous "Sermon on the Mount," found in Matthew 5–7, He didn't tell everyone to loosen up and relax, because sin was an old-fashioned concept. He didn't reassure people that God doesn't mind too much. Instead, He took some of the well-known Ten Commandments and provided an even stricter interpretation of what obedience to God's Law should be.

> You have heard that it was said to the people long ago, "You shall not murder, and anyone who murders will be subject to judgment." But I tell you that anyone who is angry with a brother or sister will be subject to judgment. Again, anyone who says to a brother or sister, "Raca," is answerable to the court. And anyone who says, "You fool!" will be in danger of the fire of hell …
>
> You have heard that it was said, "You shall not commit adultery." But I tell you that anyone who looks at a woman lustfully has already committed adultery with her in his heart. (Matthew 5:21–22, 27–28)

Many in our modern world would like to believe that Jesus simply came and preached a message of love without any moral standards.

However, as the example above showed, Jesus offered an even stricter view of morality and ethics than many in His already strict culture.

Shockingly, in our age, Jesus also talked about the reality of hell and judgment and the wrath of God.

> If your right eye causes you to stumble, gouge it out and throw it away. It is better for you to lose one part of your body than for your whole body to be thrown into hell. And if your right hand causes you to stumble, cut it off and throw it away. It is better for you to lose one part of your body than for your whole body to go into hell. (Matthew 5:29–30)

Those words came right after the warning quoted above about anyone who lusts having already committed adultery in their heart. So it seems clear that for Jesus, the consequences of breaking God's laws, even if only within your own heart, are dire.

One of my new favorite authors, Rebecca McLaughlin, writing about this passage, notes:

> Here Jesus lands two terrifying points. First, the extreme seriousness of sin—sexual and otherwise. Sin earns us all a ticket straight to hell. We're better being maimed than getting on that train. But second, if we read this in the context of Jesus' teachings as a whole, we find that it's not our eyes or our hands that cause us to sin. It's our heart. The rot has gone so deep that there's no part of us that salvageable. So, what on earth are we to do?[263]

Both of these "terrifying points" are at odds with our wider culture today.

The concept of hell is rejected as an antiquated relic of a power-hungry religious system that wanted to control people's lives. And yet as we've already seen, Jesus certainly believed in a place of eternal suffering called hell and often warned people about going there.

> Do not be afraid of those who kill the body but cannot kill the soul. Rather, be afraid of the One who can destroy both soul and body in hell. (Matthew 10:28)

Likewise, we live in a culture that rejects the idea of the sinfulness of human beings, believing in the essential goodness of humanity. But again, Jesus disagreed with that. Rather than looking within oneself and basing our identity and behavior on how we feel, Jesus warned that our feelings can lead us astray and that our hearts are incredibly evil:

> What comes out of a person is what defiles them. For it is from within, out of a person's heart, that evil thoughts come—sexual immorality, theft, murder, adultery, greed, malice, deceit, lewdness, envy, slander, arrogance and folly. All these evils come from inside and defile a person. (Mark 7:20–23)

Having said that, however, Jesus was utterly different from Jonah in that His warnings about sin and judgment and hell were not the primary focus of His teaching.

Instead, the heart of Jesus's message was an invitation to escape judgment by turning from our sin and running to Him.

His message was one of hope and forgiveness and acceptance by a holy God.

He preached a message of grace.

Jesus invited people to repent because the kingdom of heaven is near.[264]

Jesus told stories (called parables) where ordinary people are welcomed into the kingdom of God.[265]

Jesus said He had come to offer the water of eternal life.[266]

Jesus declared that those who took on His yoke and followed His teaching will find true rest.[267]

Jesus warned the hypocritical religious leaders that repentant sinners will enter the eternal kingdom ahead of them.[268]

And Jesus described God as a shepherd searching for one lost sheep, a woman scouring her home for one lost coin, and a father scanning the far horizon for a glimpse of his lost son.[269]

Jesus certainly warned people about the consequences of sin and the judgment of God. But His primary message was that He had come to offer life, both now and forever, to those who trust in Him.

> His message is clear: sin of every kind will pave our way to hell. But He will throw His arms around us if we come to Him for help.[270]

Unlike Jonah, Jesus preached a message of grace.

Jesus is Greater in His Sacrifice

So Jesus is greater than Jonah in His *obedience, compassion*, and *preaching*.

But the most important way that Jesus is greater is in His *sacrifice*.

And that is what Jesus's comment about "the sign of Jonah" is pointing to in the gospels.

Here is the key passage again by way of reminder.

> He answered, "A wicked and adulterous generation asks for a sign! But none will be given it except the sign of the prophet Jonah. For as Jonah was three days and three nights in the belly of a huge fish, so the Son of Man will be three days and three nights in the heart of the earth. The men of Nineveh will stand up at the judgment with this generation and condemn it; for they repented at the preaching of Jonah, and now something greater than Jonah is here." (Matthew 12:39–41)

Jesus here was clearly drawing a comparison between Jonah's experience in being cast overboard into the sea and being swallowed by the fish before being vomited out and what He would experience in dying and being buried before rising again.

In some ways, then, Jonah was unwittingly a prototype pointing through history to Jesus.

In Jonah 1, as the storm continued to increase in ferocity, despite the efforts of the sailors to lighten the ship or to pray or row against it, Jonah told the sailors,

> Pick me up and hurl me into the sea and it will grow calm. I know that it is on account of me that this great storm has come upon you. (Jonah 1:12)

Tim Keller points out that Jonah's command to the sailors to toss him overboard is an example of substitutionary love.[271]

He was offering his life for theirs.

I argued back in chapter 2 that Jonah could have repented and confessed his wrongdoing to Yahweh and (I am convinced) that, in response, Yahweh would have stilled the storm and allowed the sailors to take Jonah back to Joppa. But that would have meant Jonah would then have had to obey the word of Yahweh and head for Nineveh, which was something he was still not prepared to do. So his command to the sailors was more of a death-wish.

And yet he was still unwittingly offering himself as a substitute—his life for theirs.

This is part of "the sign of Jonah"—the way Jonah pointed to the coming of Jesus.

Jesus also came as a substitute, One who would offer His life in exchange for us, as numerous scriptures make clear:

> For even the Son of Man did not come to be served, but to serve, and to give his life as a ransom for many. (Mark 10:45)[272]

> Look, the Lamb of God, who takes away the sin of the world! (John 1:29)[273]

> For there is one God and one mediator between God and mankind, the man Christ Jesus, who gave himself as a ransom for all people. (1 Timothy 2:5–6)

> This is how God showed his love among us: he sent his one and only Son into the world that we might live through him. This is love: not that we loved God, but that he loved us and sent his Son as an atoning sacrifice for our sins. (1 John 4:9–10)

Even as a substitute, however, Jesus was significantly different from, and greater than, Jonah.

For example, Jesus was *an intentional substitute.*

As the quotation from Mark 10:45 above makes clear, Jesus came to this earth with the intention of offering His life as a substitute. The death of Jesus was no accident or unforeseen mistake—rather, all the gospels present Jesus predicting his death and telling His closest disciples well before it happened.[274]

Jesus came into this world with the intention of offering His life for us.

Jonah had certainly never boarded the ship planning to offer his life as a substitute for the sailors.

Jesus was also *an innocent substitute.*

There's a sense in which Jonah's offer of sacrifice was actually about his own sin and rebellion. The storm that was ravaging the ship was a result of Jonah's rebellion and disobedience, as he himself acknowledged (Jonah 1:12).

Jesus, on the other hand, was an innocent substitute. He did not suffer for His own sins or rebellion as He was without sin (Hebrews 4:15). Instead, Jesus willingly took the penalty of our wrongdoing on Himself as these ancient words from the prophet Isaiah make clear:

> Surely he took up our pain
>   and bore our suffering,
> yet we considered him punished by God,
>   stricken by him, and afflicted.
> But *he was pierced for our transgressions,*
>   *he was crushed for our iniquities;*
> *the punishment that brought us peace was on him,*
>   *and by his wounds we are healed.*
> We all, like sheep, have gone astray,
>   each of us has turned to our own way;
> and *the* LORD *[Yahweh] has laid on him*
>   *the iniquity of us all.* (Isaiah 53:4–6; emphasis added)

Finally, Jesus was *a complete substitute*. He actually suffered and died for us.

While Jonah offered his life and was thrown overboard by the sailors, he didn't die and was instead rescued by Yahweh sending the great fish.[275] Jesus, on the other hand, not only experienced physical death through crucifixion, but also endured the outpouring of God's wrath for our sin.

> Jonah only came near to death and went under the water, while Jesus actually died and came under the weight of our sin and punishment … Christ dealt with the wrath of God on sin and evil by standing in our place and bearing the punishment we deserve.[276]

Unlike Jonah, Jesus was an *intentional*, *innocent*, and *complete* substitute.

Jesus > Jonah

However, "the sign of Jonah" conveys more than just the idea of substitution.

A key part of the "sign" is the comparison between Jonah's "three days and three nights in the belly of a huge fish" and Jesus's "three days and three nights in the heart of the earth" (Matthew 12:40).

Notice what is similar and different in those phrases.

What is similar is the *time reference*—"three days and three nights."

What is different is the *location*—"in the belly of a huge fish" versus "in the heart of the earth."

Once again, Jonah was a prototype, a pointer to Jesus. While their experiences were different—Jonah was alive inside the great fish, while Jesus would die and be buried in a tomb—what they shared in common was the period of time they were missing from among the living.

By the way, the phrase "three days and three nights" was simply a Hebraic way of talking about three days. Some people get confused by that because most scholars believe that Jesus was executed on a Friday and rose again on the Sunday (think about Good Friday and Easter Sunday). However, this common Hebraic expression doesn't necessarily mean three complete days (a full seventy two hours)—it simply means a part of three consecutive days or nights.[277]

Just as Jonah ended up exiting the great fish after three days, so too Jesus would walk out of the tomb on the third day.

> Just as Jonah was thrown into the sea so that the sailors on the ship might be saved, Jesus was thrown into the depth of the earth for our redemption. He was silent for three days. Then, on the morning of the third day, God the Father took the earth in His hand and shook it, and brought His Son to life again. That was the sign of all signs, the resurrection of Christ.
>
> No sign authenticates the person of Christ more completely and powerfully than His resurrection from the dead. We simply will not get anything greater than this sign. If we will not acquiesce to it, we will not benefit from the ministry of Jesus. We will remain in the ranks of the scribes and the Pharisees, the "evil and adulterous generation."[278]

The resurrection of Jesus is the ultimate proof of both the effectiveness of His sacrifice for sin and the truthfulness of His claims to be Almighty God, Yahweh of the Old Testament.

That is why the apostle Paul argues in his famous chapter on the resurrection in 1 Corinthians 15 that without the resurrection of Jesus, the Christian faith is meaningless and false.

And if Christ has not been raised, our preaching is useless
and so is your faith. More than that, we are then found to be
false witnesses about God, for we have testified about God
that he raised Christ from the dead ... And if Christ has not
been raised, your faith is futile; you are still in your sins. Then
those also who have fallen asleep in Christ are lost. If only for
this life we have hope in Christ, we are of all people most to
be pitied. (1 Corinthians 15:14–19)

The resurrection of Jesus was key to me fully embracing Him as my
Savior and Lord. I grew up in a Christian home and trusted in Christ
at around the age of ten. But as I grew through my teenage years, like
many others, I had questions and doubts about whether this faith was
real or not.

That was when I discovered the writings of an author named Josh
McDowell.[279] His defense of the reliability of the Bible and the
person and work of Jesus was instrumental in confirming my initial
commitment to Christ.

But it was McDowell's defense of the resurrection of Jesus that was
crucial. He took Paul's words from 1 Corinthians 15 quoted above and
explained that the entire Christian faith hangs on the single thread
of the resurrection.

Prove that Jesus didn't rise from the dead, and Christianity is
obliterated.

Believe the evidence that Jesus did rise bodily from the dead, and
Christianity *must* be true.

And as McDowell helped me sift through the evidence, I became
convinced—as I still am to this day—that Jesus rose again.

The tomb is empty.

Jesus is alive.

It's all true.

Jesus is the greater substitute, the only Savior, because he walked out the grave, conquering death forever.

Jesus, Jonah, and the Day of Atonement

So why is all this important?

In the introduction to this book, I have discussed the tradition in some Jewish synagogues of reading the book of Jonah aloud on Yom Kippur—the Day of Atonement.[280] It is at the conclusion of this reading that the congregation then stands and confesses together, "We are Jonah."

Yom Kippur is the holiest day in the Jewish year.

The regulations for this day are carefully laid out in Leviticus 16. This was the only day in which the high priest could enter the holiest part of the tabernacle or temple—the holy of holies.[281] This was where the ark of the covenant was positioned as a symbol of God's presence among His people.

The high priest would bathe and offer sacrifices for his own personal sins. He would then choose two goats to be the primary actors in this holy drama, and lots would be cast between them.

One of the goats would then be sacrificed as an offering for the people's sin—that was the *substitute*.[282]

The other goat was the *scapegoat*—a term still in use today.

The high priest would lay his hands on the head of the scapegoat and confess the sins of the people publicly. This was a dramatic way of passing the sins from the people onto the scapegoat. The scapegoat would then be led out into the wilderness and released, symbolically carrying the sins of the people far, far away.[283]

Back in chapter 5, I recited the words of Psalm 103, which quotes Exodus 34 about Yahweh being a gracious and compassionate God, and then celebrates His forgiveness. Read these amazing words again, this time with the imagery of the Day of Atonement and the scapegoat carrying the sins of the people far away:

> He does not treat us as our sins deserve
> or repay us according to our iniquities.
> For as high as the heavens are above the earth,
> so great is his love for those who fear him;
> as far as the east is from the west,
> so far has he removed our transgressions from us.
> (Psalm 103:10–12)

That's the promise of the Day of Atonement.

The regulations around the Day of Atonement about the role of the two goats was another prototype pointing to Jesus.

Jesus is our *substitute*, who died in our place.

And Jesus is our *scapegoat*, who carried our sins far away.

And the reason we need a substitute, a scapegoat, a Savior?

Because of the confession that is made every year on the Day of Atonement when the story of Jonah is read.

I am Jonah.

Brad Carr

And so are you.

And because I am Jonah, I need Jesus.

Just like Jonah and the sailors and the Ninevites, you and I are incapable of dealing with our sin and atoning for our failure.

And as we reflect on the book of Jonah, we are meant to see not just Jonah's failures but also our own.

Our sin.

Our pride.

Our brokenness.

And that is not to condemn us or to weigh us down with shame but to show us how much we all need grace—pagans and prophets, Nazis and normal people.

> Jesus is the prophet Jonah should have been … [but] Jesus did not merely weep for us; he died for us. Jonah went outside the city, hoping to witness its condemnation, but Jesus Christ went outside the city to die on a cross to accomplish its salvation.[284]

That is why Jesus is the only Savior.

My prayer, as we come to the end of our exploration of this brilliant story, is that you will see not just the foibles of Jonah but also your own failures. Your foolishness in running from God, your failure to fully obey, your tendency towards selfishness and arrogance.

But more than that, my prayer is that you will see the incomparable, undeserved, amazing, life-giving, compassionate forgiveness and love of God.

May you know His grace through Jesus, and may it transform you in ever-increasing ways.

I am Jonah, so I need Jesus.

Father,

Thank You for Jesus. Thank You that because we are all Jonah, we all need Jesus.

Thank You for Jesus's perfect obedience to You. Thank You for His compassion and love for the broken. Thank You for both His teaching and example of forgiveness. Thank You that while Jesus warned us about judgment and hell, He also shared Your love and heart of forgiveness and grace.

Thank You most of all for Jesus's sacrificial death on the cross as my substitute and scapegoat. And thank You that after three days, Jesus rose again from the grave, conquering sin and death forever.

Make me more like Jesus and less like Jonah through the power and presence of Your Spirit in my life, I pray.

Amen.

Discussion Questions

1. As you read this chapter on how **Jesus** > **Jonah**, what affected you the most? Why?

2. Why do you think the religious leaders of Jesus's time demanded yet another miraculous sign from Him? Why did Jesus respond so harshly to them?

3. What impacts you most when you consider Jesus's compassion for hurting people?

4. Jesus talked very strongly about sin and judgment, and yet "sinners" flocked to Him. Why do you think Jesus was able to attract non-religious people while saying hard things about sin and evil?

5. How do you respond to the idea that Jesus is an intentional and innocent substitute for you?

6. Why is the resurrection of Jesus so crucial for the Christian faith?

7. As you consider the symbolism of the Day of Atonement, what does it mean for you that Jesus is our substitute and scapegoat if we have trusted in Him?

8. As you complete this book, what did you find most challenging or encouraging? Why?

Epilogue

Thanks for reading my story.

I understand that the risk in writing it is that people who read it may well judge me for my attitude and actions.

And to be fair, that will be perfectly understandable.

I still can't believe that I chose to disobey Yahweh and tried to run from His presence.

It's embarrassing to admit the deep selfishness, arrogance, and callousness that lurked in my own heart.

But I hope that, by now, you will have realized, dear reader, that the same sinfulness can also lurk in yours.

We, sons and daughters of Adam and Eve, have always struggled with selfishness. We often fail to obey God's call. We frequently neglect God's commands. We often only resort to prayer when we hit rock bottom. We easily take His grace in our lives for granted. And we can quickly question God's plans and get angry when things don't go our way.

We are not so different, are we?

And having finished my story, I can now say how thankful I am that Yahweh is exactly who He says He is: a compassionate and gracious God, slow to anger, and abounding in love and faithfulness.

I pray that you know His wonderful grace and compassion in your own life, even though you have never deserved it and can never repay it.

Shalom, my friend.

I am Jonah.

Acknowledgments

At the end of the acknowledgments in her book, *Jesus through the Eyes of Women*, Rebecca McLaughlin writes, "It takes a village of love to write a book. I'm thankful for my village."[285]

As I release my first book, I'm thankful for my village of love too.

Thanks to Rochelle, my gorgeous wife, who was the first reader of this book as well as the first listener to so many of my enthusiastic ideas through the years. I'm so thankful for her support and encouragement of many of my ideas (like this book) and her wisdom and tact with other ones that needed to be discarded. Her handwritten note of encouragement on the cover of draft no. 2 will be forever cherished!

Thanks to Harrison, Logan, and Jaden, our three amazing sons, for the joy, laughter, and love you each bring to our family. We are immensely proud of the three of you. Special thanks to Harrison for the work in designing the book cover.

Thanks to my parents, Max and Ruth Carr, and my other parents, Rowland and Elaine Forman, for the incredible support and encouragement you have poured onto Rochelle and me for all these years. Thanks for the way each of you have individually encouraged me in the writing of this book.

Thanks to my reading team, who read early drafts and gave much-needed encouragement and suggestions for improvement—Rochelle Carr, Max Carr, Rowland Forman, Reuben Munn, Drew Leaver,

Thealyssa Ng, and Jonathan Dove. If you're reading this book and there's anything you disagree with, blame one of them!

Thanks to David Hall for casting his detailed editorial eye over the entire book. I am so grateful for your God-given skills.

Thanks to Kevin Harney for agreeing to write the foreword, and for blessing many pastors and leaders in New Zealand over the past decade. I'm personally so grateful for what Kevin and his wife, Sherry, have poured into my life through their teaching, writing, and examples.

Thanks to the congregation, staff, and elders of Summit Church (now Gracecity East), for the joy of leading and serving with you for sixteen great years. This book was born as a preaching series at Summit, and the encouragement I received from these fantastic people inspired me to make Jonah's story the subject of my first book.

Thanks also to the congregation, staff, and board of Gracecity Central. I felt loved and welcomed as I stepped into a teaching role with you all, and teaching Jonah in another church setting was the impetus I needed to keep going with the writing project.

Thanks to my "band of brothers" (and sisters) who gathered around me in love and compassion during my months of burnout in 2019 and who continue to walk the road with Rochelle and me. Special shoutout here to Tim and Bronwyn Collins, Jonathan and Robyn Dove, Harataki and Shona Manihera, Nick and Sarah Field, Miles (and the late Margaret) Davison, Igor and Hannah Gerritsen, Reuben and Anna Munn, Robin and Sonia Byrne, and the many other friends and colleagues throughout New Zealand.

Thanks to the board members of Barnabas School of Leadership and

Living Stones Network, whom I have served alongside for a number of years.

Thanks to our faithful financial supporters and prayer partners who support and care for us in this new season of ministry.

Thanks to our border collie, Arlo, for getting Rochelle and me out the door every morning for a long walk.

And most of all, thank you, Jesus, for showering me with undeserved grace and unfailing love, especially in all those moments when I am still forced to admit "I am Jonah."

Appendix: "I Am Jonah" Statements

I am Jonah.

I am Jonah when I say no to what God has clearly said.

I am Jonah when I resist God altering my life plans.

I am Jonah when I fail to talk to God.

I am Jonah when I would rather be comfortable than obedient.

I am Jonah when I assume I can run from God.

I am Jonah when I forget that my sin affects others' lives.

I am Jonah when my life doesn't measure up to what I say I believe.

I am Jonah when God saves others in spite of me, rather than because of me.

I am Jonah when my prayer life often revolves around moments of crises.

I am Jonah when I can quote the Bible but don't put it into practice.

I am Jonah when I arrogantly look down on sinners instead of humbly reflecting God's grace.

I am Jonah when I fail to acknowledge the depth of my sin.

I am Jonah when I accept God's grace, but my attitude hasn't really changed.

I am Jonah when I obey God, but my heart isn't really in it.

I am Jonah when I only communicate one aspect of the biblical message.

I am Jonah when I get angry at God for not doing what I want.

I am Jonah when I try to sit in judgment of God.

I am Jonah when I think I'm better than I really am.

I am Jonah when my comfort is more important than God's mission.

I am Jonah when I love things more than people.

I am Jonah when I forget how deeply God loves sinners.

I am Jonah when I am grateful for God's forgiveness but unwilling to forgive others or to help them find forgiveness.

I am Jonah, so I need Jesus.

Recommended Resources

Allen, Leslie. *The Books of Joel, Obadiah, Jonah, and Micah: The New International Commentary on the Old Testament*. Grand Rapids, MI: Eerdmans Publishing, 1976.

Bridges, Jerry. *Transforming Grace: Living Confidently in God's Unfailing Love*. Colorado Springs, CO: NavPress, 1991, 2008.

Bruckner, James. *Jonah, Nahum, Habakkuk, Zephaniah: NIV Application Commentary*. Grand Rapids, MI: Zondervan, 2004.

Comer, John Mark. *God Has a Name*. Grand Rapids, MI: Zondervan, 2017.

Keller, Timothy. *The Prodigal Prophet: Jonah and the Mystery of God's Mercy*. London, UK: Hodder and Stoughton, 2018.

Nixon, Rosemary. *The Message of Jonah: The Bible Speaks Today*. Nottingham, UK: InterVarsity Press, 2003.

Sklar, Jay. "Jonah." In *ESV Expository Commentary, vol. 7: Daniel–Malachi*, 387-422. Wheaton, IL: Crossway, 2018.

Youngblood, Kevin. *Jonah: God's Scandalous Mercy: Hearing the Message of Scripture Commentary Series*. Grand Rapids, MI: Zondervan, 2013.

Endnotes

Introduction: A Great Story

1. "If we look into Jonah's mirror we will also see ourselves." Richard D. Phillips, *Jonah and Micah*, Reformed Expository Commentary (Phillipsburg, NJ: P&R Publishing Company, 2010), 13.

2. Rosemary Nixon, *The Message of Jonah: The Bible Speaks Today* (Nottingham, UK: InterVarsity Press, 2003), 39–41.

3. J. D. Greear, *The Gospel According to Jonah: A New Kind of Obedience* (Nashville, TN: LifeWay Press, 2013), 5.

4. For more, see the epilogue in Timothy Keller, *The Prodigal Prophet: Jonah and the Mystery of God's Mercy* (London, UK: Hodder and Stoughton, 2018), 227–28.

5. For example, the prophets Hosea, Isaiah, and Jeremiah immediately spring to mind.

6. See 2 Kings 14:25.

7. Kelly M. Kapic, *You're Only Human: How Your Limits Reflect God's Design and Why That's Good News* (Grand Rapids, MI: Brazos Press, 2022), 199–200.

8. Leland Ryken, *Words of Delight: A Literary Introduction to the Bible* (Grand Rapids, MI: Baker Book House, 1993), 337.

9. Ron Allen, *Jonah and Ruth* online course, Dallas Theological Seminary, accessed May 7th 2020, https://courses.dts.edu/register/jonah-ruth/.

10. See Robert Chisholm Jr., *Interpreting the Historical Books: An Exegetical Handbook* (Grand Rapids, MI: Kregel Publications, 2006), 86–87.

11. The exception is Jonah 1:17 in our modern versions, which should probably be read as the opening verse of chapter 2. This is how it is numbered in the Tanakh, the Hebrew Bible, where it is actually Jonah 2:1, with chapter 1 having sixteen verses and chapter 2 having eleven. For more information, see chapter 3, "A Great Prayer."

12. See especially Douglas Stuart, *Hosea – Jonah: Word Biblical Commentary, vol. 31* (Nashville, TN: Thomas Nelson, 1988), 435–442.

13   See Exodus 13:17 – 14:31.

14   See Joshua 10:1–15.

15   There are a number of scholars who speculate that Jonah might be a parable rather than a true story, similar to the parables that Jesus used in His teaching ministry. However, a close reading of the book suggests that it doesn't read this way. Parables generally were brief (normally involving a simple scene or two), used anonymous characters who were not real, and were obviously fictional in the way they were told. Jonah, however, is presented as a real historical figure who is verified elsewhere in the historical record of the Bible (2 Kings 14:25), and the complex storyline has different scenes and references to real people and places. See the helpful discussion by Douglas Stuart in *The Dictionary of Old Testament Prophets* as he convincingly argues that Jonah should not be understood as a parable, allegory, or midrash. Douglas Stuart, "Jonah, Book of," in *The Dictionary of Old Testament Prophets* (Downers Grove, IL: Inter-Varsity Press, 2012), 458.

      In addition, it seems that Jesus believed the story of Jonah was true. Jesus referred to "the sign of the prophet Jonah" in at least two instances in the gospels (see Matthew 12:39–42 and 16:1–4; see also Luke 11:29–32). He also linked his future bodily resurrection to the events in Jonah (we'll explore this more in chapter 7 of this book). In the context of that teaching, Jesus talked about the people of Nineveh who responded to Jonah being at the last judgment at the end of time. As Dr. Craig Blomberg points out, this makes the idea that Jonah is simply a parable unlikely. "It makes no sense to say that mythical people will be part of the final judgment" (Craig Blomberg, *Can We Still Believe the Bible? An Evangelical Engagement with Contemporary Questions* [Grand Rapids, MI: Brazos Press, 2014], 157). Hence, I do not believe it's necessary to read the book of Jonah as an extended parable.

16   T. Desmond Alexander, "Jonah: An Introduction and Commentary," in *Obadiah, Jonah and Micah: The Tyndale Old Testament Commentaries Series*, ed. D. J. Wiseman (Leicester, UK: Inter-Varsity Press, 1988), 73. Writing about the great fish, he notes, "The author's portrayal of this most peculiar event is very low key; it has certainly not been included in order to heighten the dramatic quality of the narrative. This being so, why would the author have invented it, if it did not really happen?" (111–112).

17   G. Campbell Morgan. Quoted by Matt Smethurst in his interview with Timothy Keller for the Gospel Coalition. Matt Smethurst, "Tim Keller

on a Fishy Story," The Gospel Coalition, U. S. Edition, October 3, 2018, https://www.thegospelcoalition.org/article/tim-keller-fishy-story/.

Chapter 1: A Great Call

18   The full list in order in our modern Bibles is Hosea, Joel, Amos, Obadiah, Jonah, Micah, Nahum, Habakkuk, Zephaniah, Haggai, Zechariah, and Malachi. Because of their shorter length, they were placed all together onto one scroll, and commonly called "the Twelve."

19   A "life verse" is a verse of the Bible that is chosen by someone as summing up their purpose, identity, or hope as a follower of Jesus.

20   While others such as Isaiah, Jeremiah, and Hosea have some narrative portions, those books are mainly prophecies written in poetic form. The only other prophetic book that does contain significant narrative portions is that of Daniel, which is split almost evenly between narrative and prophecy. Interestingly, in the Hebrew Bible, Daniel ended up in the section called "Writings," separate from the other prophets, whereas Jonah remained in the prophetic section.

21   In addition to Hosea, the prophetic books of Jeremiah, Ezekiel, Joel, Micah, Zephaniah, Haggai, Zechariah, and Malachi all start with similar words.

22   In addition to introducing prophetic books, the formula *"the word of Yahweh"* is used many more times through the writings and ministries of the prophets. Here are just a few examples: Elijah in 1 Kings 17:2, 8 and 18:1; Elisha in 2 Kings 7:1; Isaiah in 2 Kings 20:4, 16 and Isaiah 1:10, 38:4, 66:5; Jeremiah in Jeremiah 1:4, 2:1 as well as Ezra 1:1 and Daniel 9:2; Ezekiel in Ezekiel 6:1; Amos in Amos 7:16; Haggai in Haggai 1:3, 2:1; and Zechariah in Zechariah 4:6, 8, 6:9; etc. These are just a small sampling of biblical references.

23   See, e.g., Genesis 15:1,4; Exodus 9:20–21; 19:7; Deuteronomy 5:5; 1 Samuel 3:7, 15:10; 2 Samuel 7:4; and 1 Kings 6:11.

24   Terence Fretheim, "Yahweh" in *New International Dictionary of Old Testament Theology and Exegesis (NIDOTTE) vol. 4,* ed. Willem A. VanGemeren (Grand Rapids, MI: Zondervan, 1997), 1295.

25   I am following the example of John Mark Comer in his outstanding book, *God Has a Name* (Grand Rapids, MI: Zondervan, 2017). See the comment on page 12 of his book.

26   Phil Moore suggests that Jonah might have become a national hero due to this prophecy, recognized as a "big-shot prophet." See Phil Moore, *Straight to the Heart of the Minor Prophets* (Oxford, UK / Grand Rapids, MI: Monarch Books, 2017), 85.

27   Stuart, *Hosea – Jonah*, 431.

28   Keller, *The Prodigal Prophet*, 12.

29   "The commissioning of a prophet to visit and to preach to a foreign nation was unprecedented in Hebrew prophecy." Kevin Youngblood, *Jonah: God's Scandalous Mercy: Hearing the Message of Scripture Commentary Series* (Grand Rapids, MI: Zondervan, 2013), 53.

30   His prophecy against Assyria is in Isaiah 10:5–19, while an entire portion of Isaiah's book, from chapter 13 to chapter 23 contains prophecies against Babylon, Philistia, Moab, Damascus, Cush, Egypt, Edom, Arabia, and Tyre, as well as Judah and Jerusalem.

31   See Amos 1:3 – 2:3 for his prophecies against Damascus, Philistia, Tyre, Edom, Ammon, and Moab. Similarly, Jeremiah would announce oracles against Egypt, Philistia, Moab, Ammon, Edom, Damascus, Kedar, Hazor, Elam, and Babylon in chapters 46 – 51 of his book.

32   The quote and many details are from Bruckner, *Jonah, Nahum, Habakkuk, Zephaniah*, 28–30.

33   Quoted in Bruckner, *Jonah, Nahum, Habakkuk, Zephaniah*, 29.

34   Quoted by Nixon, *The Message of Jonah*, 63.

35   The dating of the book of Nahum is debated. Several scholars place Nahum a century *before* Jonah's time. See Keller, *The Prodigal Prophet*, 14, n.7; and Leslie C. Allen, *The Books of Joel, Obadiah, Jonah and Micah: The New International Commentary on the Old Testament* (Grand Rapids, MI: William Eerdmans Publishing Company, 1976), 190.

     However, it seems more likely that Nahum prophesied about a century *after* Jonah, after the overthrow of the city of Thebes in Egypt, which is alluded to in Nahum 3:8–10. See Richard D. Patterson, *Nahum, Habakkuk, Zephaniah: The Wycliffe Exegetical Commentary*, ed. Kenneth Barker (Chicago, IL: Moody Press, 1991), 3–7; and Tremper Longman III, "Nahum," in *The Minor Prophets: An Exegetical and Expository Commentary*, ed. Thomas Edward McComiskey (Grand Rapids, MI: Baker Academic, 2009), 766–768.

36   Jay Sklar, "Jonah" in *ESV Expository Commentary, vol. 7: Daniel–Malachi* (Wheaton, IL: Crossway, 2018), 397.

[37] See the article by J. A. Thompson, "Tarshish," in *New Bible Dictionary*, 2nd ed. (Leicester, UK: InterVarsity Press, 1982), 1165. "Tarshish was at the other end of the world from Nineveh." Allen, *Joel, Obadiah, Jonah, and Micah*, 204. See also Bruckner, *Jonah, Nahum, Habakkuk, Zephaniah*, 42.

[38] Allen, *Joel, Obadiah, Jonah, and Micah*, 204.

[39] Kevin Youngblood even suggests a possible chiasm (inverted structure) for verse 3, as follows:

> A. Jonah got up to flee **to Tarshish**, <u>away from Yahweh's presence</u>
>> B. <u>He descended</u> to Joppa
>>> X. He found a ship **bound for Tarshish** and paid its fare
>> B' <u>He descended</u> into it
> A' to accompany them **for Tarshish**, <u>away from Yahweh's presence</u>

See Youngblood, *Jonah*, 51.

[40] It is not absolutely certain that Jonah would have known Psalm 139, but the heading of the psalm records that it was a psalm of David, so it would have been circulating among God's people for around four hundred years. Additionally, as we will see in chapter 3, Jonah's prayer/psalm in the belly of the fish shows a tremendous awareness and knowledge of the book of Psalms as the hymnbook of the people of God.

[41] Youngblood, *Jonah*, 51–58.

[42] Greear, *The Gospel According to Jonah*, 11.

[43] Colossians 4:3.

[44] Revelation 3:8.

[45] Youngblood, *Jonah*, 59.

[46] See Keller, *The Prodigal Prophet*, 17–21.

[47] Priscilla Shirer, *Life Interrupted: Navigating the Unexpected* (Nashville, TN: B&H Publishing Group, 2011), 11.

[48] Keller, *The Prodigal Prophet*, 15.

[49] 1 Thessalonians 5:17.

[50] Moore, *Straight to the Heart of the Minor Prophets*, 85.

Chapter 2: A Great Storm

[51] As I said in the introduction, my belief is that Jonah was probably the author of the book that bears his name.

52 See for example, 1 Samuel 18:11 and 20:33. Youngblood, *Jonah*, 60.

53 See https://nzhistory.govt.nz/keyword/cook-strait.

54 See the article on Wikipedia at https://en.wikipedia.org/wiki/Cook Strait.

55 Sklar, "Jonah," 400.

56 See Mark 4:35–38.

57 See chapter 7, "A Greater Jonah," for more on the contrast between Jonah and Jesus.

58 The irony of this moment is heightened by the fact that the captain used the same verb that Yahweh did in verse 2 – "arise" or "get up" (*qum* in Hebrew). Yahweh commanded Jonah to "get up and go…" and now the captain called him to "get up and pray…" Jonah chose to disobey them both. See Bruckner, *Jonah, Nahum, Habakkuk, Zephaniah*, 44.

59 See Matthew 27:35.

60 John Goldingay, *Hosea – Micah: Baker Commentary on the Old Testament Prophetic Books* (Grand Rapids, MI: Baker Academic, 2021), 383.

61 Leviticus 16:8–10.

62 Numbers 26:55-56, 33:54, 34:13, 36:2: Joshua 14:2, 18:8–10, 19:51.

63 Luke 1:7.

64 Acts 1:26.

65 Genesis 3:13, 12:18, 26:10, 29:25 and Exodus 14:11.

66 Youngblood, *Jonah*, 79.

67 Allen, *Joel, Obadiah, Jonah, and Micah*, 209.

68 See Keller, *The Prodigal Prophet*, 32–33.

69 See Goldingay, *Hosea – Micah*, 382.

70 Ibid., 384.

71 Youngblood, *Jonah*, 82.

72 Keller, *The Prodigal Prophet*, 64.

73 Verse 17 should be read as the first verse of the next chapter; see chapter 3 for more details.

74 Allen, *Joel, Obadiah, Jonah and Micah*, 212; Michael B. Shepherd, *A Commentary on the Book of the Twelve: The Minor Prophets* (Grand Rapids, MI: Kregel Publications, 2018), 224.

75   "This [verse 16] can hardly be something less than whole-hearted conversion to Yahweh: as already noted, the phrase '*to fear/revere* God' in the OT consistently describes those who have and maintain a healthy relationship with Yahweh. The sailors' sacrifices and vows in the same verse confirm this, since such actions habitually prove a permanent commitment to a deity." Daniel C. Timmer, *A Gracious and Compassionate God: Mission, Salvation and Spirituality in the Book of Jonah: New Studies in Biblical Theology*, vol. 26 (Nottingham, UK: Apollos / Inter-Varsity Press, 2011), 73.

76   James Bruckner persuasively argues that Yahweh's pursuing love is central to chapter 1. See Bruckner, *Jonah, Nahum, Habakkuk, Zephaniah*, 50.

77   Timmer, *A Gracious and Compassionate God*, 75.

Chapter 3: A Great Prayer

78   I found the cartoon on Pinterest at https://www.pinterest.nz/pin/429390145722515502/ (accessed September 15, 2021). If you're interested to see the cartoon, you can also Google "Gary Larsen Jonah."

79   According to the website Blue Letter Bible, paragraphs were added in the fifth century by the scholar Jerome in the Vulgate, his translation of the Bible into Latin. Chapters were then put in place in 1227 by Prof. Stephen Langton, a future archbishop of Canterbury. Finally, verses were added as early as AD 900 in the Hebrew Bible by the Ben Asher family and were standardized by a French printer, Robert Stephanus, in 1551. The Geneva Bible (1560) was the first English Bible to use chapters and verses as we know them today. See Don Stewart, "Why Is the Bible Divided into Chapters and Verses?" *Blue Letter Bible*, accessed Feb 9th, 2023, https://www.blueletterbible.org.

80   For example, most commentators on Genesis agree that the first chapter of Genesis should include the first three verses of chapter 2 and that Genesis 2:4 is the beginning of the second creation story as suggested by the "toledot" heading, "This is the account of the heavens and the earth." See Kenneth Mathews, *Genesis 1–11*, The New American Commentary (Nashville, TN: Broadman and Holman Publishers, 1996), pp.113–115. "The chapter break is usually deemed inappropriate since the description of the creative week continues until 2:3," 176.

81   See Bruckner, *Jonah, Nahum, Habakkuk, Zephaniah*, 50.

[82]   Some commentators still make this claim. For example, Richard Phillips in the Reformed Expository Commentary on Jonah and Micah, uses a key heading in his chapter, "Jonah's Prayer of Deliverance." He assumes that *"the belly of Sheol"* in verse 2 is the belly of the fish, and then states, "Jonah saw his delivering fish as a kind of prison, fast shut with the tightest of bars." Richard D. Phillips, *Jonah and Micah: Reformed Expository Commentary* (Phillipsburg, NJ: P&R Publishing Company, 2010), 78–79.

As much as I enjoyed his commentary in many places, however, I believe that this author has missed several key aspects of the text. For example, nowhere does he note the past tense language that Jonah used. Furthermore, while he acknowledges the quotations and allusions to several psalms, he fails to appreciate how many of those psalms are songs of thanksgiving.

[83]   Goldingay, *Hosea – Micah*, 386.

[84]   Bruckner, *Jonah, Nahum, Habakkuk, Zephaniah*, 82.

[85]   Youngblood, *Jonah*, 105.

[86]   Shepherd, *A Commentary on the Book of the Twelve*, 226–227.

[87]   Youngblood, *Jonah*, 96-102, especially figure 4.2 on the poetic structure of Jonah 2 on page 100.

[88]   Shepherd, *A Commentary on the Book of the Twelve*, 227.

[89]   See Matthew 12:38-41 and Luke 11:29-32.

[90]   Vernon McGee, "Jonah: Dead or Alive?", *Blue Letter Bible*, accessed September 15, 2021, https://www.blueletterbible.org.

[91]   I also believe they have misunderstood the parallel that Jesus was drawing out in the gospels, but we will look at that in chapter 7.

[92]   Kenneth Barker, "Praise" in *Cracking Old Testament Codes*, ed. by D. Brent Sandy and Ronald L. Giese Jr. (Nashville, TN: Broadman and Holman Publishers, 1996), 227.

[93]   Youngblood, *Jonah*, 107.

[94]   Bruckner, *Jonah, Nahum, Habakkuk, Zephaniah*, 75.

[95]   Goldingay, *Hosea – Micah*, 391.

[96]   Allen, *Joel, Obadiah, Jonah, and Micah*, 219.

[97]   See, for example, Youngblood, *Jonah*, 113; Timmer, *A Gracious and Compassionate God*, 88.

[98]   Sklar, "Jonah," 410.

99   Ibid.

100   Nixon, *The Message of Jonah*, 150.

101   Ibid., 151.

102   Keller, *The Prodigal Prophet*, 81.

103   Rosemary Nixon makes a great point about the obedience of each of these elements that Yahweh provided. "On each occasion the creature responds obediently to the voice of its Creator. The contrast with Jonah's response is clear, and the irony plain." Nixon, *The Message of Jonah*, 125.

104   Allen, *Joel, Obadiah, Jonah, and Micah*, 220.

105   Eg. Leviticus 18:25–28, 20:22; Isaiah 19:14, 28:8. See Youngblood, *Jonah*, 114.

106   Youngblood, *Jonah*, 111.

107   Timmer, *A Gracious and Compassionate God*, 81-82.

108   Keller, *The Prodigal Prophet*, 6-7.

109   That is the meaning of the father's commands in the parable to clothe his son in the best robe (which would have been the father's one) with a ring on his finger and sandals on his feet (Luke 15:22). It is a beautiful description of the wonder of God's grace.

110   All quotations taken from Paul E. Miller, *A Praying Life: Connecting with God in a Distracting World* (Colorado Springs, CO: NavPress, 2009), 14–16.

111   J. I. Packer and Carolyn Nystrom, *Praying: Finding Our Way through Duty to Delight* (Downers Grove, IL: IVP Press, 2006), 17.

112   Phillips, *Jonah and Micah*, 76.

113   Quoted by current Dallas Seminary president Mark Yarbrough in his book, *How to Read the Bible Like a Seminary Professor* (New York, NY: FaithWords, 2015), xv. Hendricks wrote something similar in his book *Living By The Book*, although it is not the exact phrase. Howard Hendricks and William Hendricks, *Living by the Book* (Chicago, IL: Moody Press, 1991), 31.

114   Hendricks, *Living by the Book*, 292-301.

115   Kevin Harney, *Leadership from the Inside Out: Examining the Inner Life of a Healthy Church Leader* (Grand Rapids, MI: Zondervan, 2007), 14–18.

116   Ibid., 16–17.

117 This section on mediating on God's Word is taken from *The SaLT Course*, a leadership development curriculum that I have developed for churches. See Brad Carr, *SaLT Course – Semester One, Heart: The Character of a Leader*, 2022, 100–101.

118 Moore, *Straight to the Heart of the Minor Prophets*, 86.

119 Sklar, "Jonah," 410.

120 D. A. Carson, "Sin's Contemporary Significance," in *Fallen: A Theology of Sin*, ed. Christopher W. Morgan and Robert A. Peterson (Wheaton, IL: Crossway, 2013), 34.

121 Jerry Bridges, *Respectable Sins: Confronting the Sins We Tolerate* (Colorado Springs, CO: NavPress, 2007), 16.

122 Ibid., 19–20.

Chapter 4: A Great City

123 See the parable in Matthew 25:14–30, that the NIV entitles, "The Parable of the Bags of Gold."

124 See Exodus 2-4.

125 See John 21:15–19. The story of Peter's denial of Jesus is recorded in all four of the New Testament gospels; see Matthew 26:69–75; Mark 14:66–72; Luke 22:54–62; John 18:15–18 and 25–27.

126 For the story of Paul's hunting of early followers of Jesus, see Acts 8:1–3 and 9:1–2, as well as his later reflections in 1 Timothy 1:15–17. The story of Paul's conversion is found in Acts 9:1–19 and retold in Acts 22:1–21 and 26:2–23.

127 Shirer, *Life Interrupted*, 127.

128 Youngblood, *Jonah*, 122.

129 "Chapter 3 mirrors the action of chapter 1." Bruckner, *Jonah, Nahum, Habakkuk, Zephaniah*, 88.

130 See, among others, Sklar, "Jonah," 412; Allen, *Joel, Obadiah, Jonah, and Micah*, 220.

131 See Numbers 20:1-13.

132 See 2 Chronicles 26:16-21.

133 See Acts 5:1-11.

134 Galatians 6:7.

135   See especially Exodus 34:6–7, which is quoted numerous times throughout the rest of the Old Testament, as we will see in the next chapter.

136   Youngblood, *Jonah*, 126.

137   See chapter 1 for more details on the cruelty and terror of the Assyrian empire.

138   Bruckner, *Jonah, Nahum, Habakkuk, Zephaniah*, 90.

139   Michael Shepherd is one commentator who prefers this translation. See Shepherd, *A Commentary on the Book of the Twelve*, 230.

140   See Youngblood, *Jonah*, 131, n.1.

141   Youngblood goes even further than this, and argues that the phrase should be translated as, "Now Nineveh was a great metropolis *belonging to God*" (emphasis his). However, that idea seems too strong. It is probably better seeing this as a statement of the city's *value* to God, rather than His personal ownership. See Youngblood, *Jonah*, 131.

142   See John 3:16.

143   James Montgomery Boice, *The Minor Prophets, vol. 1, An Expositional Commentary, Hosea – Jonah* (Grand Rapids, MI: Baker Books, 1983), 296.

144   Kevin Youngblood points out that neither the *origin* of the divine message, nor the *grounds* of the prophesied judgment, are clearly spelled out in Jonah's preaching. See Youngblood, *Jonah*, 133.

145   Ibid., 134.

146   Daniel Timmer is a good example of this position. In his book on the theology of the book of Jonah, he spends several pages exploring why he believes the Ninevites repentance does not mean they turned to Yahweh in faith. He concludes, "Where does all this leave us? Nineveh believed in God, turned from her sin in some degree, but did not fully turn to God. In other words, her repentance was partial and incomplete." Timmer, *A Gracious and Compassionate God*, 104.

147   Keller, *The Prodigal Prophet*, 89.

148   Ibid.

149   However, I'm not alone in drawing that conclusion. For example, Jay Sklar writes, "The people of Nineveh believed it (the message)! The phrase '*believed God*' is used elsewhere to describe Israelites who put their faith and trust in the Lord (Gen. 15:6; Ex. 14:31), and that is what happened here. The entire city believes Jonah's God is living and real, and therefore

they turn to him with humble repentance" (Sklar, "Jonah," 413). Also, Shepherd, *A Commentary on the Book of the Twelve*, 231–32.

150   Nixon, *The Message of Jonah*, 166.

151   See Romans 4:3 and Galatians 3:6.

152   Youngblood, *Jonah*, 135.

153   Ibid.

154   Goldingay, *Hosea – Micah*, 397.

155   Leslie Allen suggests this was a Persian custom to include animals in ceremonies of mourning, since the same animals would have shared in the destruction of judgement if it came. Allen, *Joel, Obadiah, Jonah and Micah*, 224.

156   Kevin Youngblood points out that this question about whether God may do something is a rhetorical feature that is used ten times in the Old Testament (see eg. Esther 4:14). However, this is the only time out of the ten occurrences when the speaker is a Gentile rather than a member of God's covenant people. Youngblood, *Jonah*, 140.

157   Goldingay, *Hosea – Micah*, 399.

158   Youngblood, *Jonah*, 139.

159   Sklar, "Jonah," 414.

160   Allen, *Joel, Obadiah, Jonah, and Micah*, 224.

161   Several commentators point to a series of events in eighth-century Assyria that may have made the people of Nineveh more spiritually attune to the preaching of a visiting prophet. For example, Daniel Timmer talks about government instability, famines, plagues, revolts, and eclipses as events that may have created a spiritually attentive environment for Jonah (see Timmer, *A Gracious and Compassionate God*, 93-94).

However, as Youngblood points out, "The narrative refuses to give any credit for Nineveh's repentance to secondary causes... The narrative keeps the readers' attention firmly fixed on the divine word as the only cause. Nineveh's remarkable repentance is therefore attributable to nothing but the power of God's word" (Youngblood, *Jonah*, 142).

162   See esp. Nahum 3:1–3. The prophecy of conquest was fulfilled in 612 BC by the Babylonians. See Daniel C. Timmer, "Nahum" in *ESV Expository Commentary, vol. 7: Daniel – Malachi* (Wheaton, IL: Crossway, 2018), 505–06.

[163] Allen, *Joel, Obadiah, Jonah, and Micah*, 226.

[164] Wayne Grudem, *Systematic Theology: An Introduction to Biblical Doctrine* (Leicester, UK: Inter-Varsity Press, 1994), 163.

[165] Ibid., 203.

[166] See 1 Peter 1:18–21. Revelation 13:8 describes Jesus as "the Lamb who was slain from the creation of the world."

[167] See Romans 5:6–8, Ephesians 5:1–2, and 1 Peter 2:21–25.

[168] D. A. Carson, *Scandalous: The Cross and Resurrection of Jesus* (Wheaton, IL: Crossway, 2010), 67.

[169] Phillips, *Jonah and Micah*, 95, 98.

[170] Hugh Martin, *A Commentary on Jonah*, quoted in Phillips, *Jonah and Micah*, 96, 99.

[171] It is true that in one sense Christians are *positionally* already sanctified – that is, in trusting in Jesus by faith, we are already "sanctified in Christ Jesus" (see Acts 20:32; 1 Corinthians 1:2, 6:11) and "set apart" in holiness. However, the Bible is also very clear that we are also *being* sanctified as the Holy Spirit transforms us throughout our lifetime. This idea of *progressive* sanctification is how the word is normally understood.

[172] Gregg R. Allison, *50 Core Truths of the Christian Faith: A Guide to Understanding and Teaching Theology* (Grand Rapids, MI: Baker Books, 2018), 265–66.

[173] See 2 Corinthians 3:18.

[174] See 2 Corinthians 8–9, esp. 9:6–9.

[175] See Psalm 84, esp. vv.1–2.

[176] See Psalm 119, esp. vv.47–48.

[177] See Matthew 6:1–18.

[178] See, for example, Ephesians 2:1–10.

[179] Jerry Bridges, *Transforming Grace: Living Confidently in God's Unfailing Love* (Colorado Springs, CO: NavPress, 1991, 2008), 40.

Chapter 5: A Great Anger

[180] You can watch the video on YouTube at https://www.youtube.com/watch?v=jO2QsF_nnIU (accessed November 30, 2021). You can also find more of their fantastic resources at http://crossroadskidsclub.net/

181   Keller, *The Prodigal Prophet*, 97–98.

182   Timothy Keller, *Counterfeit Gods: When the Empty Promises of Love, Money, and Power Let You Down* (London, UK: Hodder and Stoughton, 2009), 143.

183   Comer, *God Has a Name*, 137.

184   Sklar, "Jonah," 417.

185   Bruckner, *Jonah, Nahum, Habakkuk, Zephaniah*, 109.

186   Old Testament scholar Leslie Allen captures the play on words between these three uses of *ra'ah* (in 3:8 – 4:1) when he paraphrases the passage using the English word 'bad': "*Bad* behaviour should lead to a *bad* end, and Jonah takes it very *badly* that it does not." Allen, *Joel, Obadiah, Jonah, and Micah*, 227.

187   Bruckner, *Jonah, Nahum, Habakkuk, Zephaniah*, 109.

188   Youngblood, *Jonah*, 152.

189   Keller, *The Prodigal Prophet*, 20-21.

190   See chapter 1 for more details on the atrocities that the ancient Ninevites were guilty of.

191   Greg Haslam, *The Jonah Complex: Rediscovering the Outrageous Grace of God* (Shippensburg, PA: Destiny Image Publishers, 2014), 43, 45.

192   Dan B. Allender, *Leading with a Limp: Turning Your Struggles into Strengths* (Colorado Springs, CO: Waterbrook Press, 2006), 16.

193   Ibid., 102.

194   Comer, *God Has a Name*, 32. I highly recommend this superb treatment on the name and character of Yahweh in Exodus 34.

195   See my forthcoming book, *Our God: Exploring the Character of God in the Story of the Exodus*, for an exposition of this passage and the rest of the book of Exodus.

196   Tim Chester, *Exodus for You: God's Word for You Series* (Epsom, UK: The Good Book Company, 2016), 237.

197   W. Ross Blackburn, *The God Who Makes Himself Known: The Missionary Heart of the Book of Exodus, New Studies in Biblical Theology*, vol. 28, ed. D. A. Carson (Downers Grove, IL: InterVarsity Press, 2012), 153.

198   It is quoted in part or in full in Numbers 14:18; 2 Chronicles 30:9; Nehemiah 9:17, 31; Psalms 86:15, 103:8, 111:4, 112:4, 145:8; Joel 2:13; and Nahum 1:3. In addition, key phrases or words from this passage are used dozens of times through the Old Testament.

199 Comer, *God Has a Name*, p.32 (emphasis his).

200 "The recurrence of the verb 'to pray' connects this prayer to the one Jonah uttered from the fish's belly (2:2). These are the verb's only two occurrences in the book, and they invite comparison of Jonah's prayers. Ironically, the same mercy that inspired Jonah's praise when he was saved also provokes his complaint when Nineveh was saved." Youngblood, *Jonah*, 152.

201 Jay Sklar rightly suggests that Jonah "displays a shocking depth of self-centered blindness." Sklar, "Jonah," 417.

202 We have already noted Jonah's death wish in chapter 1 when he refused to pray to Yahweh or repent of his stubborn rebellion and would rather be thrown into the stormy sea.

203 Allen, *Joel, Obadiah, Jonah, and Micah*, 229; Goldingay, *Hosea – Micah*, 401. Interestingly, Kevin Youngblood draws a comparison between Jonah and Moses in Exodus 32–34, where Moses interceded for the nation of Israel and offered to lay his life on the line (Exodus 32:32). However, I think a link between Jonah and Moses is much more tenuous than the more obvious connection to Elijah. See Youngblood, *Jonah*, 155–6.

204 Elijah's story is found in 1 Kings 17 – 2 Kings 2.

205 Allen, *Joel, Obadiah, Jonah, and Micah*, 229.

206 In the "I Am Jonah" reflections at the end of chapter 1, I noted Tim Keller's observation that Jonah exhibits traits of both the younger and elder sons from Jesus's famous parable about the two sons in Luke 15. What that means, of course, is that Yahweh in the book of Jonah functions like the loving father in the parable, who graciously and deliberately searches for both of his sons.

207 Mark Vroegop, *Dark Clouds, Deep Mercy: Discovering the Grace of Lament* (Wheaton, IL: Crossway, 2019), 28.

208 Ibid., 21.

209 Vroegop adds, "You might think lament is the opposite of praise. It isn't. Instead, lament is a path to praise as we are led through our brokenness and disappointment… Think of lament as the transition between pain and promise." Ibid.

210 The story is found in Jeremiah 18.

211 Keller, *The Prodigal Prophet*, 139.

212 Vroegop, *Dark Clouds, Deep Mercy*, 29.

213 Ibid., 74, 79.

214 See Malachi 4:5. Jesus affirmed in the New Testament that John the Baptizer was this prophesied forerunner, the Elijah figure who was to come (see Matthew 11:14, 17:10–13; Luke 1:17).

215 Matthew 17:1–13.

216 See Mark 8:28.

217 See 1 Samuel 15, especially verses 30–31.

218 See Acts 5:1–11. Note carefully the word "also" in 5:1, which ties their decision to sell a piece of property back to actions of Joseph in 4:36–37. This man Joseph, the text notes, was nicknamed Barnabas ("son of encouragement") by the apostles. Perhaps Ananias and Sapphira were hoping for nicknames of their own!

219 Philippians 2:3.

220 Romans 12:3.

Chapter 6: A Great Lesson

221 "Yahweh responds to Jonah's anger with an object lesson designed to trap Jonah in his own theological inconsistency." Youngblood, *Jonah*, 161.

222 See Stuart, *Hosea – Jonah*, 50; also, Goldingay, *Hosea – Micah*, 402.

223 Sklar, "Jonah," 418.

224 The musical was made into a movie in 2012 by Universal Pictures starring Hugh Jackman and Anne Hathaway. I highly recommend it.

225 Allen, *Joel, Obadiah, Jonah, and Micah*, 232.

226 James Bruckner assumes a vine without comment; see Bruckner, *Jonah, Nahum, Habakkuk, Zephaniah*, 113–114. Likewise, Douglas Stuart simply talks about a gourd; see Stuart, *Hosea – Micah*, 505.

227 Youngblood, *Jonah*, 169.

228 Allen, *Joel, Obadiah, Jonah, and Micah*, 233.

229 Bruckner, *Jonah, Nahum, Habakkuk, Zephaniah*, 116.

230 Keller, *The Prodigal Prophet*, 118.

231 Ibid., 118–120.

232 The Hebrew word "*chus*," translated "pity" in verse 17, is the same word that Yahweh uses in Jonah 4:10–11.

233 Shepherd, *A Commentary on the Book of the Twelve*, 236.

234 See, for example, Deuteronomy 28:14; Joshua 1:7; and 2 Chronicles 34:2.

235   Boice, *The Minor Prophets 1*, 309.

236   Stuart, *Hosea – Micah*, 507.

237   Nixon, *The Message of Jonah*, 199–200.

238   I am indebted to Kevin Youngblood for describing this aspect of the contrast so well. See Youngblood, *Jonah*, 172.

239   Sklar, "Jonah," 419.

240   See Allen, *Joel, Obadiah, Jonah and Micah*, 235; Sklar, "Jonah," 419-420; Moore, *Straight to the Heart of the Minor Prophets*, 105.

241   Sinclair B. Ferguson, *Man Overboard! The Story of Jonah* (Edinburgh, UK: Banner of Truth Trust, 2008), 98.

242   Words and music by Brooke Ligertwood, © 2006 Hillsong Music Publishing Australia (Rest of World) & Sony/ATV Music Publishing Australia (Aus/NZ Only) CCLI: 4785835.

243   See Acts 8:1–3, 9:1–2, as well as Pauls' own comments in 1 Timothy 1:12–14.

244   See Acts 9:1–16, 22:3–21, 26:4–18.

245   Craig Blomberg, *Neither Poverty or Riches: A Biblical Theology of Possessions: New Studies in Biblical Theology.*, vol. 7, ed. D. A. Carson (Leicester, UK: Apollos Press, 1999), 132.

246   Randy Alcorn, *The Treasure Principle: Discovering the Secret of Joyful Living* (Sisters, OR: Multnomah Publishers, 2001), 42–43 (emphasis his).

247   Moore, *Straight to the Heart of the Minor Prophets*, 105.

248   Grant Osborne, *Matthew: Zondervan Exegetical Commentary on the New Testament*, ed. Clinton Arnold (Grand Rapids, MI: Zondervan, 2010), 694.

249   Ibid.

250   Ibid., 696.

251   Kevin G. Harney, *Organic Outreach for Ordinary People* (Grand Rapids, MI: Zondervan, 2009), 26.

Chapter 7: A Greater Jonah

252   Osborne, *Matthew*, 482.

253   I am indebted to Michael Shepherd for this insight. Shepherd, *A Commentary on the Book of the Twelve*, 218.

254   This criterion is found in Deuteronomy 18:22.

255 Shepherd, *A Commentary on the Book of the Twelve*, 218 (emphasis added).

256 The examples of the tax collectors Matthew and Zacchaeus stand out here. Matthew (also called Levi) was a tax collector in Capernaum (Mark 2:13–14) who became one of the twelve apostles and the author of the first gospel. Zacchaeus was "a chief tax collector" in Jericho whom Jesus specifically sought out despite his sin (Luke 19:1–10). Tax collectors were hated for both their dishonesty and their collaboration with the despised Romans. The label "tax collector" was itself a term of abuse and hatred, and often linked with "prostitutes" (Matthew 21:31–32) or "sinners" (Luke 15:1) by other Jews. See "Taxes," T. E. Schmidt, *Dictionary of Jesus and the Gospels*, ed. Joel Green, Scot McKnight, and I. Howard Marshall (Downers Grove, IL: InterVarsity Press, 1992), 804–807.

257 For example, after Jesus invited Matthew (Levi) to follow Him as a disciple-student, Matthew threw a great party in honour of Jesus and invited all the people he knew, meaning other tax collectors and sinners. The religious leaders who observed Jesus' behaviour were horrified that He would associate with people like that (Mark 2:15–17). In the case of Zaccheaus, it was not only the religious leaders, but "all the people" who muttered about Jesus's association with this hated man (Luke 19:7).

258 In John 4, Jesus initiated a conversation with a Samaritan woman who had come out to the village well to draw water in the heat of the day (John 4:1–42). Not only was she surprised that He, a Jewish man, spoke to her as a Samaritan and a woman (see verse 9), but His disciples were also shocked to find Him speaking to a woman when they returned from the nearby village (verse 27).

259 Perhaps the most controversial example is with a woman in Luke's gospel who is unnamed, but who is simply described as "a woman ... who lived a sinful life" (Luke 7:37). She anointed Jesus's feet with costly perfume, probably as an act of worship (see the reference to her great love in verse 47). However, the religious leader hosting the dinner party was scandalized that Jesus allowed the woman to even touch Him (verse 39). Jesus then added to the scandal by announcing to her that her sins were forgiven (verse 48).

260 In addition to the Samaritan woman in John 4, Jesus attracted and welcomed Gentiles from places like the Decapolis and Tyre-Sidon – they were in the crowds that came to Him for teaching and healing (Mark 3:8 and Luke 6:17). He also willingly engaged with other individual Gentiles such as the Roman centurion who asks for healing for his servant (Matthew 8:5–13),

the demon-possessed man in the mainly-Gentile Gerasenes (Mark 5:1–20), and a Canaanite woman in Tyre as well as a deaf and mute man in the Gentile area of the Decapolis (two stories told side-by-side in Mark 7:24–37). There is some debate over the story of the Canaanite woman in Tyre as Jesus seemed to harshly refer to Gentiles as "dogs," (Mark 7:27), a common Jewish insult of Gentiles. However, it is likely that Jesus "is being deliberately provocative, seeking to draw out a response of persistent faith from the woman." See Mark Strauss, *Mark: Zondervan Exegetical Commentary on the New Testament* (Grand Rapids, MI: Zondervan, 2014), 313.

261 Luke 23:39–43. This example, and the wording, was suggested by my dad, Max Carr, who served as one of my early readers. Thanks Dad.

262 Matthew 28:18–20 and Acts 1:8.

263 Rebecca McLaughlin, *Confronting Jesus: 9 Encounters with the Hero of the Gospels* (Wheaton, IL: Crossway, 2022), 104.

264 Mark 1:14–15.

265 Matthew 22:1–14.

266 John 4:13–14.

267 Matthew 11:28–30.

268 Matthew 21:31–32.

269 Luke 15:1–32.

270 McLaughlin, *Confronting Jesus*, 112.

271 See his extended discussion in Keller, *The Prodigal Prophet*, 60-66.

272 The original text uses the preposition "*anti*" meaning "for," and it clearly conveys the idea of substitution. "The prevailing sense for *anti* … is '*instead of, in place of*,' conveying the idea of substitution" (Joel Williams, *Exegetical Guide to the Greek New Testament: Mark* [Nashville, TN: B&H Academic, 2020], 180). See also the discussion by Strauss, *Mark*, 458–59; and Keller, *The Prodigal Prophet*, 64.

273 Describing Jesus as "the Lamb of God" has deep roots in the Old Testament, where lambs were often sacrificed as substitutes for people. See chapter 8, "Jesus the Sacrifice" in McLaughlin, *Confronting Jesus*, 149-167.

274 Mark's gospel, for example, has Jesus predicting His death and resurrection at least three times – Mark 8:31–33; 9:3–32; and 10:32–34.

275 As noted back in chapter 3, there is a small number of commentators and preachers who argue that Jonah did in fact die, either by drowning in the

sea, or later inside the great fish. For example, Pastor Greg Haslam writes, "Jonah's departure into the deep and the confines of the sea monster's belly was not a temporary swoon or a limp, near-death experience. We need to understand that he actually died... When Jonah prays as recorded in chapter 2 verses 1-9, he is praying as a disembodied spirit, a dead soul. He is finished, his body is drowned, and he is lifeless at the bottom of the sea" (Haslam, *The Jonah Complex*, 118).

The primary reasons that Haslam and others hold to this minority view is (1) they read the poetic language of Jonah 2 too literally, especially the reference to descending to "the realm of the dead" or "Sheol" (Jonah 2:2); and (2) they believe the comparison to Jesus in Matthew 12 and elsewhere only works if Jonah actually died. However, they actually misread the text on both points. First, I explained back in chapter 3 that the reference to Sheol is poetic in just the same way as David used it in Psalm 18:2–3. No one argues that David died during the events that he was describing – he was using poetic language to depict how close he came to death, just as Jonah was doing in Jonah 2 inside the great fish. Second, Jesus never said that Jonah died, and the comparison being drawn was not about death. The key part of Jesus's comparison is about time – "three days and three nights." The idea that Jonah died is not supported by a close reading of the text.

276   Keller, *The Prodigal Prophet*, 63, 65.

277   For example, in the Old Testament book of Esther, she called on her uncle to pray for three days and nights as she prepared to enter the presence of the king unannounced (Esther 4:16). However, just a few verses later, she went in to see the king "on the third day" (Esther 5:1-2). Therefore, when she asked for prayer, Esther wasn't necessarily saying they had to fast for a full seventy-two hours before she would approach the king. It was simply an expression suggesting a period of three days.

Jesus did the same thing in the gospels. While He talked about "three days and three nights" in Matthew 12, at other times He predicted that He would die and *on the third day* would rise again (e.g., Matthew 16:21). See Norman Geisler and Thomas Howe, *The Big Book of Bible Difficulties* (Grand Rapids, MI: Baker Books, 1992), 343.

278   R. C. Sproul, *Matthew: St. Andrews Expositional Commentary* (Wheaton, IL: Crossway, 2013), 399–400.

[279] His two most influential books in my life were *Evidence That Demands a Verdict* and *The Resurrection Factor*, both of which are still in print today. See Josh McDowell, *The New Evidence That Demands a Verdict* (Nashville, TN: Thomas Nelson, 1999) and Josh McDowell, *The Resurrection Factor* (Milton Keynes, UK: Authentic Media, 2005).

[280] Bruckner, *Jonah, Nahum, Habakkuk, Zephaniah*, 127.

[281] Leviticus 16:2.

[282] Leviticus 16:9.

[283] Leviticus 16:20.

[284] Keller, *The Prodigal Prophet*, 124.

Acknowledgments

[285] Rebecca McLaughlin, *Jesus Through the Eyes of Women: How the First Female Disciples Help Us Know and Love the Lord* (Austin, TX: The Gospel Coalition, 2022), 180.

Printed in the United States
by Baker & Taylor Publisher Services